3000 Power Words
and Phrases *for* Effective
Performance Reviews

3000

Power Words *and* Phrases *for* Effective PERFORMANCE REVIEWS

Ready-to-Use Language for Successful Employee Evaluations

SANDRA E. LAMB

TEN SPEED PRESS
Berkeley

Copyright © 2013 by Sandra E. Lamb

All rights reserved.
Published in the United States by Ten Speed Press, an imprint of the
Crown Publishing Group, a division of Random House, Inc., New York.
www.crownpublishing.com
www.tenspeed.com

Ten Speed Press and the Ten Speed Press colophon are registered trademarks of
Random House, Inc.

Library of Congress Cataloging-in-Publication Data
Lamb, Sandra E.
3,000 power words, phrases, and sentences for effective performance reviews /
by Sandra E. Lamb. — First edition.
    pages cm
Includes index.
1. Employees—Rating of. 2. Employees—Rating of—Terminology. I. Title.
HF5549.5.R3L34 2013
658.3'125014—dc23
                         2013017501

Trade Paperback ISBN: 978-1-60774-482-5
eBook ISBN: 978-1-60774-483-2

Printed in the United States of America

Design by Colleen Cain

10 9 8 7 6 5 4 3 2 1

First Edition

Contents

SECTION FOUR

SECTION FIVE

*The difference between the almost right word
and the right word
is the difference between the lightning bug
and the lightning.*

—SAMUEL CLEMENS

INTRODUCTION
The Value of Power Words

Amy (let's call her) has an office next to the corner office, which is occupied by her boss, whom we'll call Ted. Both Ted and Amy have been in these offices for three years. The two share a common wall; and they frequently overhear telephone conversations the other is having while negotiating with a client or coworker.

Ted and Amy go to all the same product release and sales meetings. They see each other in the elevator and break room; and sometimes they casually chat about upcoming holidays, how Ted's children are doing in school, or the general state of the national and international economies.

Ted likes Amy and feels that she's doing a good job as district sales manager. The strange thing here is that Ted has, for the entire three years he's been Amy's boss, communicated with her for work assignments, updates, progress reports, general information, and even for her performance reviews, entirely by email. He has not conducted a single face-to-face encounter to discuss how she is performing in her role as district sales manager. In short, Ted is clueless about his role as supervisor.

Clearly, Ted either feels entirely unqualified to conduct a face-to-face meeting, or he suffers from a fear of confrontation—or both. He seems to feel that doing an in-person performance review, or directly discussing other situations with Amy, offers the possibility that an unpleasant confrontation could occur. She could disagree with his assessment. She could challenge him. So Ted avoids such encounters.

While Ted is meeting his own personal goal of avoiding a possible confrontation, he is not meeting his responsibility as a supervisor/manager. Privately, he admits that he was unprepared for this role, and it's one he's not comfortable in. Avoiding a face-to-face meeting with Amy is his way of trying to dodge this part of his job.

But he is doing Amy, and their company, a severe disservice.

The result of Ted's failure to have a face-to-face review is that Amy doesn't feel she has any real connection to Ted, nor does she feel a sense that they are teammates working together to achieve common corporate goals. In fact, the absence of this vital part of the review process has meant that Amy hasn't gotten the feedback she needs to perform at her full potential, nor has she gotten vital input that would help her set her future career goals. She doesn't know how she's performing in her sales manager role within the organization as a whole.

Hopefully, Ted will buy a copy of this book. And when he follows the simple steps in these pages, he will be able to easily overcome his fear of conducting meetings with Amy. This book will give him the tools—the exact power words—to do his job of manager efficiently and expertly.

It will help Amy, too. Following the simple steps in this book will mean that Ted, Amy, and their organization will all perform at a much higher level.

Rethink Traditional Annual Performance Reviews

THE DEBATE STILL RAGES: does the annual performance review offer real value, or does it alienate employees from their managers? The answer is, of course, it all depends. Survey results indicate that the once-a-year review, when used as the only performance measurement tool, fails miserably to make lasting performance improvements. But when it is part of an overall performance improvement program, it can be very effective.

The proper framework for all performance reviews is that the employee and manager first focus on the big-picture objectives: (1) increasing customer benefits and satisfaction; (2) adding value to the organization; and (3) contributing to the efforts of the team or coworkers.

For any performance system to work at its best, the relationship between manager and employee needs to be one of mutual respect, support, and collaboration. Rather than being a disciplinarian, the manager needs to be a performance coach. Then, of course, there's the issue of timing. The function of performance coach works best when done on an ongoing basis—daily, once a week, biweekly, or once a month. This approach means that whenever the more formal performance reviews are scheduled, the employee will not be surprised by how his performance is rated.

The most productive manager/employee relationships are based on a dialogue, not a monologue. That means that the employee feels comfortable enough to initiate communication with his manager and to contribute to and offer his own input on his performance. Doing this on an ongoing basis offers the best possibility for performance improvement.

The successful manager will regularly

- **Connect the employee's daily performance to the organization's goals and values**
- **Reinforce positive behavior; give employees feedback regularly and on the spot, using positive recognition to underscore positive behavior**
- **Review real performance and corrects negative behaviors (before they become bad habits)**
- **Set goals—in concert with the employee—for growth, and develops strategies, steps, and time frames for reaching them**
- **Motivate**

Get Ready—Before the Performance Review

Create a System of Measurement

The first item of business is that the organization needs to establish a system of measurement to assess the employee's performance in terms of quality, quantity, cost, timeliness, and impact on other employees. This will make the review step in the performance process most beneficial. A three-level scoring method of "needs improvement," "average," or "excellent" used by the manager at the end of each year doesn't offer the employee real guidance.

Surveys indicate that a six-level rating system works better:

- 5 is Outstanding (O), Excellent (E), or Far Exceeded Standards (FES)
- 4 is Exceeded Standards (ES), or Good (G)
- 3 is Met Standards (MS), or Average (A)
- 2 is Below Standards (BS), or Needs Improvement (NI)
- 1 is Far Below Standards (FBS), Poor (P), or Unsatisfactory (U)
- 0 is Not Observed (NO), Not Ratable (NR), Not Applicable (NA), or Failed (F)

Used in concert with this six-level system, or independently, some organizations find that a numerical scale that shows percentage of the highest score ("arrives for work on time 75 percent of the time") or a system that ranks performance in each area on a 1 to 10 scale works well. The numerical systems may also use an overall score to measure each employee's total performance.

Quantifiable evaluations help employees improve. Consider this evaluation: "Your attendance record shows that you arrive at work on time 40 percent of the time. This needs to improve. You need to get that number to above 90 percent. What on-time attendance target can we set for the next three months?" Quantifying like this is far more effective than giving a simple "Needs improvement" rating.

Using a more precise scale puts teeth in the measurement process and helps the employee set incremental goals for improvement. Each organization must set its own metrics for measurement.

Using this scale, set levels for performance in each area to the demands of the employee's job description. Here are some words that might be used to express each level of performance.

⑤ Outstanding (O), Excellent (E), Far Exceeded Standards (FES)

- Aced
- Always
- Bang-up
- Best
- Brilliant
- Delivered every time
- Eclipsed
- Exceeded
- Excelled
- Exceptional
- Exemplary
- First class
- First rate
- Great
- Head and shoulders above
- Never failed
- Outdid
- Outperformed
- Outshined
- Outstanding
- Peerless
- Perfect
- Second to none
- Splendid
- Stand-out
- Superb
- Supreme
- Surpassed
- Transcended
- Trumped
- Unequaled
- Unparalleled
- Upstaged

④ Exceeded Standards (ES), Good (G)

- Able
- Above average
- Accomplished
- Consistently
- Continually
- Customarily
- Dependable
- Frequently
- Habitually
- Often
- Oftentimes
- Ordinarily
- Performed well
- Proficient
- Repeatedly
- Routinely exceeded standard performance
- Sustained a high level of performance
- Time and again
- Usually
- Well above average

❸ Met Standards (MS), Average (A)

- ❑ At grade
- ❑ Average performance
- ❑ Fulfilled the job requirements
- ❑ Half the time
- ❑ Median
- ❑ Met standards
- ❑ Normally
- ❑ Not noteworthy
- ❑ Okay
- ❑ Performed at an acceptable level
- ❑ Performed to expectations
- ❑ Routinely
- ❑ Undistinguished
- ❑ Unremarkable

❷ Below Standards (BS), Needs Improvement (NI)

- ❑ Below average performance
- ❑ Erratic
- ❑ Fails to perform at an acceptable level
- ❑ Infrequently
- ❑ Intermittent
- ❑ Irregular
- ❑ Must improve
- ❑ Now and then
- ❑ Patchy results
- ❑ Sporadic
- ❑ Spotty
- ❑ Underachieved
- ❑ Underperformed
- ❑ Uneven

❶ Far Below Standards (FBS), Poor (P), Unsatisfactory (U)

- ❑ Almost never
- ❑ Far below acceptable level
- ❑ Hardly ever
- ❑ Infrequently
- ❑ Rarely
- ❑ Scarcely
- ❑ Seldom
- ❑ Seriously underperformed
- ❑ Unacceptable performance

⓿ Not Observed (NO), Not Ratable (NR), Not Applicable (NA), Failed (F)

- ❑ At no time
- ❑ Botched
- ❑ Bungled
- ❑ Completely unacceptable
- ❑ Failed
- ❑ Failing grade
- ❑ Inadequate
- ❑ Never
- ❑ No effort
- ❑ Not at any time
- ❑ Not observed/ applicable/ratable
- ❑ Not once
- ❑ Totally deficient
- ❑ Unsuccessful
- ❑ Zero score

Set Goals and Set the Stage

Setting goals is an important first step in improving performance. This does require some self-awareness on the employee's part and some analysis and guidance from the manager to determine how much improvement in what time frame can and should realistically be targeted. It's best to use an organization-wide metrics system that gives the employee quantifiable degrees of improvement for which to aim. The manager's role includes helping to define the kinds of support and training the employee may need to reach each targeted level, and making it available.

Goals are helpful to

- **Improve critical work processes and procedures**
- **Raise core skill levels, personal skills, and modify personality traits through training**
- **Reduce errors in quality**
- **Build stronger customer/client relationships and partnerships**
- **Improve peer and departmental relationships and coordination**
- **Increase innovation in work methods and processes**

Use Positive Reinforcement and Recognition

The value of using positive reinforcement can't be overemphasized. Praising the employee while he is doing something well goes a long way toward improving his overall performance. It helps the employee to self-correct and generally raises morale and motivates. It also reduces the need to emend bad behavior. Use this on an ongoing basis, along with positive recognition for improvement and work well done, to garner the best results.

EMPLOYEE PERFORMANCE IMPROVEMENT CYCLE

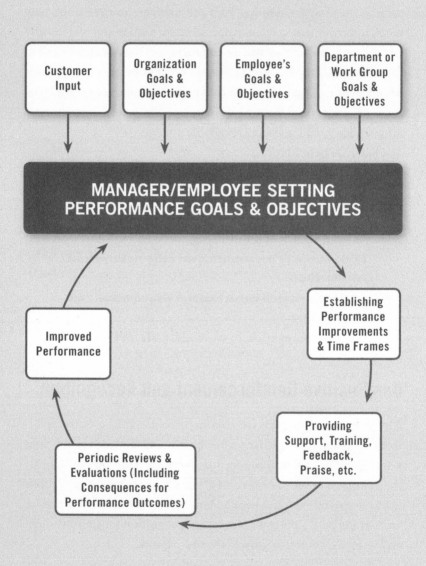

Customer Input

Organization Goals & Objectives

Employee's Goals & Objectives

Department or Work Group Goals & Objectives

MANAGER/EMPLOYEE SETTING PERFORMANCE GOALS & OBJECTIVES

Establishing Performance Improvements & Time Frames

Providing Support, Training, Feedback, Praise, etc.

Periodic Reviews & Evaluations (Including Consequences for Performance Outcomes)

Improved Performance

Time the Performance Reviews

Setting a schedule of monthly, quarterly, semiannual, or yearly performance reviews will depend upon the job and the employee's performance. Reviews should be frequent enough to help the employee and manager perform their jobs optimally in today's rapidly changing and challenging workplace. Regardless of when performance reviews are set, ongoing collaboration and discussions between the manager and the employee are needed to help the employee continue to make progress and achieve increasingly higher performance levels and job satisfaction.

Keep and Use Performance Records

It's important that all performance reviews demonstrate the organization's practice of providing fair and accurate evaluations. Before each new review, you should carefully examine the employee's prior performance reviews as a point of reference and benchmark against which progress is measured.

Use your employee journal and previous employee performance records during the review to cite examples of both good behavior and behavior that needs improvement. Be candid and explicit, and use constructive criticism where necessary. It's important that the organization's records show a pattern of careful documentation of employee reviews, and counseling, where needed. The records should include—in clear, objective language—your observations, praise, counseling, and any corrections or warnings given to the employee, along with the dates and any corrective actions taken.

Avoid legally actionable statements and references. Do not include vague or derogatory language; and do not include references to age, gender, race, or other prejudicial terms.

PERFORMANCE REVIEW INPUTS

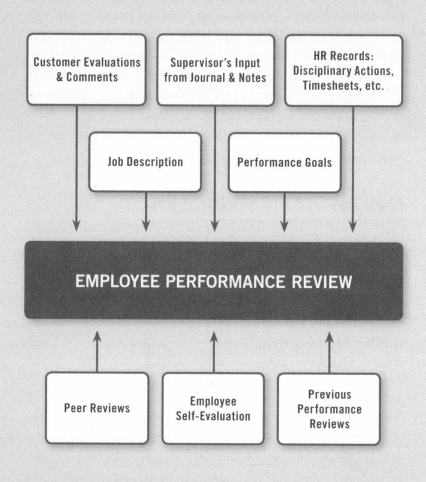

Customer Evaluations & Comments

Supervisor's Input from Journal & Notes

HR Records: Disciplinary Actions, Timesheets, etc.

Job Description

Performance Goals

EMPLOYEE PERFORMANCE REVIEW

Peer Reviews

Employee Self-Evaluation

Previous Performance Reviews

Other objective records should also be used to back up your conclusions; things like attendance records, production reports, and disciplinary reports are examples. You must be clear about how your conclusions were reached.

It's important to keep a complete and accurate record in the rare event of legal action by a terminated employee. It's also important to note that raises should not be given to employees performing at a marginal level, since a history of raises can be used in a legal dispute to argue that the employee was doing a good job.

Adjust Job Descriptions

Ultimately, the employee's job description is the standard upon which the performance review is based. The pace of business and changing roles of employees dictate that job descriptions must be modified periodically. Each modification needs to be reviewed and agreed upon by you and the employee, and the written job description needs to be altered to reflect the new scope of duties.

Use a Pre-Review Self-Evaluation

It can be beneficial to have the employee complete a self-evaluation as part of the performance review. This helps the employee take responsibility for his performance, invests him in the process, and gives him a real stake in making sure improvement occurs. Cross-departmental, subordinate(s), and customer/client evaluations should also be used, where appropriate, to help ensure objective and complete evaluations.

Make Face-to-Face a Part of the Process

A face-to-face meeting should be a part of every performance review. It helps to promote a supervisor/employee connection, build the relationship, and promote the partnership between you and the employee.

Nonverbal communication during the face-to-face review process is as important as the verbal exchange—often more important. It can help create openings for further discussion. And for the employee and manager who are reading the cues of the other person, it can promote real dialogue.

Listen before Speaking

Really hearing what the speaker—employee or manager—is saying during the performance review is key to having an effective outcome. To be an effective manager, listen carefully for clues during the employee's self-evaluation. These can trigger questions asked by the manager, to clarify and expand on what the employee has said in order to get to core issues. Careful listening will give you the opportunity to create dialogue that can springboard into making significant improvements.

Assess the Employee's Listening

It's the manager's responsibility to help the employee listen effectively, too. After giving each item of review, you should ask key questions:

- **What do you think about that?**
- **What's your response?**
- **Do you understand?**

- **Do you agree?**
- **Do you have anything to add?**

Questions like these should be followed up by other questions or statements that both put the employee at ease and help him to express his opinion. This will go a long way toward making the process effective. Ask enough key questions to be sure the employee understands, and be sure to get his input. If you discern that the employee doesn't agree but isn't saying so, you might ask, "I'm sensing you don't agree; what would you like to say about that?" or "If you believe this is inaccurate, please say so." While it's important for you to control the review process, it's also vital that you discuss each item until you and the employee can agree on setting a new goal for the next performance time frame.

Connect and Cooperate

The manager and employee should form a partnership aligned to the organization's planned outcomes and the employee's professional development. Getting to that place of consensus or connecting—mutual understanding and agreement between you and the employee—is key. It requires that you and the employee have mutual respect and support, a mutual commitment to reach a common goal, careful listening and comprehension skills, and the desire and will to improve. An effective performance review that is part of a well-planned and well-orchestrated performance management program will go a long way toward making that mutual effort happen.

When the performance review is conducted to accurately measure performance against the job description, past performance, and performance goals, the review becomes an effective management tool.

The Performance Review Process

THE PERFORMANCE REVIEW is an opportunity for you and the employee to examine his performance over the review period, identify areas where he has improved, recognize that improvement, examine areas where improvements need to be made, explore areas where additional training is needed, and set goals for future growth and development. As stated in section two, many organizations find it beneficial to use pre-review self-evaluations completed by the employee, reviews by customers and clients, and reviews by peers to help make the process complete, objective, and more informative.

The steps for the manager in the review process will usually include these:

1. **Collect performance documents.** Use the employee's job description, your own manager's journal and recorded notes, evaluations by clients and customers, evaluations by other department personnel who interface with the employee, peer reviews, the employee's self-evaluation, attendance records, HR records about disciplinary actions, and so on.

2. **Use the organization performance review form(s) and procedure(s).** Evaluate each performance dimension in light of the performance documents and your observations. Record your score for each area on the organization forms using real numbers and concrete examples to illuminate the scoring for the employee. Remember that this process should be designed to give praise as well as point out areas for improvement.

3. **Weight more heavily the skills that are most important to the successful performance of this job.** Give more consideration to the areas that are essential to the employee performing his job well, and highlight them for special emphasis during the performance review. These items should be given a higher percentage of the total score in evaluating how the employee is performing overall. If you decide to give an "Outstanding," or top score, for example, select applicable statement(s) from the lists provided, or adapt them from the lists, and include examples to support the statement(s). Use hard numbers and facts of evidence to back up your evaluation whenever possible.

   For individual skills or characteristics, assign a percentage value that reflects the employee's level of achievement.

This should be consistent with the standard used throughout the organization.

4. **Consider any training, classes, and other sources of help for the employee.** To help the organization meet its goals, and help the employee develop and grow, investigate what you may be able to recommend during the performance review and implement afterward.

5. **Meet with your manager and/or HR or other personnel.** Discuss your evaluation on the performance review form with your manager, or any other person designated by your organization's review protocol. Come to an agreement about the ratings and review as a whole.

6. **Notify the HR department or correct management member if disciplinary action or corrective action is being recommended.** Most organizations require that the manager review his employee evaluations with the HR department before the manager/employee review meeting. The small business owner may want to review his evaluation with an attorney who specializes in labor laws to avoid any illegal reference to race, gender, age, issues of discrimination, and so on.

7. **Allow the employee to review your evaluation scores.** It is helpful to allow the employee to review the performance evaluation forms before you sit down for the formal review. This gives the employee an opportunity to reflect on the evaluation and be prepared to discuss it; and it eliminates the possibility of the employee feeling ambushed or blindsided. During the face-to-face performance review meeting, make sure the employee has an opportunity to give his input on each evaluation point that is made.

8. **Conduct the performance review.** A few practical steps will help both manager and employee:

 - Meet in a quiet, comfortable, private location that will be free of interruptions.
 - Set adequate time for the review, and tell the employee ahead of time how much time it will take.
 - Sit in neutral positions at a table or in chairs side by side.
 - Speak conversationally, put the employee at ease, and keep your comments positive, whenever possible.
 - Review each item in order, emphasizing performance, and backing up your points with work examples and objective records.
 - Keep the focus on patterns of behavior and results; don't cite isolated examples.
 - Use numbers from the performance documents to make your points.
 - Allow the employee time to give his input, but don't let the review wander into unrelated matters; remain in control and keep the discussion on point.
 - Listen carefully and summarize what the employee says to be sure you have understood.
 - Respond to the employee's objections and disagreements, but don't be defensive.
 - Strive to act as a performance coach, not a disciplinarian.
 - Outline training that is available to help the employee improve and advance.
 - Help the employee set goals for performance improvement with time frames; both you and the employee should record them for future reference.
 - Have the employee sign the performance review form.
 - End the review on a positive and supportive note.

Evaluate Personal Skills, Core Competencies, and Personality Traits

THE MOST DIFFICULT IMPROVEMENT for any employee to make is to change personal bad habits that he has developed over his lifetime. This includes things like always being late; maintaining a cluttered, disorganized work area; or being unable to adapt quickly to changes in the work environment. Often these are also the most difficult for the employee to recognize and admit. Using examples of performance from objective records and observations will help underscore the points here, and setting incremental goals for improvement within defined time frames are key to helping him make effective changes.

Ability to Adapt and Make Changes

This skill is much more important for some jobs than others, but every employee needs to be able to make changes when circumstances, procedures, and policies change.

❺ Outstanding (O)

- ❏ Maintained focus and composure when things changed
- ❏ Adapted very quickly to changes in procedures
- ❏ Initiated smart changes in procedures when needed
- ❏ Showed exceptional ability to innovate and change when things weren't working
- ❏ Displayed leadership skills and calmed those around him when stresses occurred in the work environment
- ❏ Looked constantly for ways to increase productivity
- ❏ Thought clearly in a crisis and improved things that were going badly
- ❏ Handled expertly several ongoing tasks simultaneously
- ❏ Took constructive criticism well and quickly made changes
- ❏ Showed the ability to anticipate outcomes and make changes to avoid problems
- ❏ Demonstrated the ability to handle diverse responsibilities
- ❏ Embraced change as an opportunity

❹ Exceeded Standards (ES)

- ❏ Showed versatility in handling regular assignments
- ❏ Was often able to maintain focus and composure during times of change
- ❏ Performed well while juggling several assignments
- ❏ Was able to construct steps for changing procedures if given adequate time
- ❏ Took the initiative sometimes in suggesting changes to procedures that weren't working optimally
- ❏ Managed to handle stress that his subordinates found difficult

- ❑ Implemented changes with ____% success
- ❑ Transitioned into new procedures with minimum difficulty
- ❑ Accepted change well
- ❑ Was usually receptive to constructive criticism
- ❑ Exhibited a team-player spirit when new procedures had to be implemented

❸ Met Standards (MS)

- ❑ Performed at job description level
- ❑ Acclimated to changes in procedures and policies given time to process
- ❑ Did occasionally identify a more efficient way of doing a procedure
- ❑ Grappled with receiving constructive criticism
- ❑ Worked best from a strict schedule
- ❑ Could occasionally multitask
- ❑ Maintained acceptable level of calm with coworkers and subordinates
- ❑ Accepted changes passed down from upper management but sometimes needed help implementing
- ❑ Preferred established and routine operation; resisted deviations
- ❑ Faced stresses in the workplace with determination

❷ Below Standards (BS)

- ❑ Was reluctant to embrace changes in procedures
- ❑ Performed at the lower end of job description duties
- ❑ Resisted implementation of new practices and procedures
- ❑ Did not avail himself of new training programs available
- ❑ Demonstrated frustration with work interruptions
- ❑ Needed assistance in maintaining a calm work environment
- ❑ Overreacted to stress, causing disruption among coworkers and subordinates

- ❏ Refused team efforts if she determined they were not strictly within her job description
- ❏ Did not initiate time-saving and work-saving procedures even when the old ones were failing
- ❏ Tended to blame others when problems occurred

❶ Far Below Standards (FBS)

- ❏ Resisted changes in procedures
- ❏ Showed extreme stress and loss of concentration when the unexpected occurred
- ❏ Was often unable to adapt to changes in procedures and policies, even with some support
- ❏ Lost concentration and ability to keep work flowing when faced with interruptions
- ❏ Was unable to mediate flare-ups and conflicts among subordinates and coworkers in the work environment
- ❏ Instigated conflicts among subordinates and/or colleagues
- ❏ Demonstrated intolerance and inflexibility in adapting to change
- ❏ Delayed the start of training programs within the department
- ❏ Delegated work and then interfered with completion

❶ Not Observed (NO), Not Ratable (NR), Not Applicable (NA), Failed (F)

- ❏ Did not require this skill
- ❏ Refused changes in procedures
- ❏ Stonewalled when asked to participate in training programs
- ❏ Committed to deadlines and failed to keep them ____% of the time
- ❏ Failed to coordinate with peers and other departments
- ❏ Demonstrated inability to function in his present role
- ❏ Displayed unacceptable performance
- ❏ Failed to adapt as required in her job description

- Review the steps listed at the end of this section (see page 171) and include any that are appropriate.

- Ask the employee to establish relationships with peers in two related departments to review new procedures.

- Require the employee to complete and submit a production schedule for each week that reflects the ability to make changes.

Attendance and Punctuality

The employee who can be depended upon to be at work on time every day is golden. Since reliability is essential to the successful function of any enterprise, be sure this attribute receives adequate attention in the performance review.

⑤ Outstanding (O)

- ❑ Was 100% reliable in attendance and punctuality
- ❑ Showed exceptional attendance record
- ❑ Had perfect attendance record
- ❑ Performed in an extraordinary manner during departmental meetings
- ❑ Accrued distinguished attendance record
- ❑ Came to meetings fully prepared and always arrived on time
- ❑ Set a fine example for attendance and punctuality for coworkers and subordinates
- ❑ Was always prepared to begin work on time
- ❑ Displayed conscientious efforts in always meeting work deadlines
- ❑ Performed beyond the scope of the job description in making sure all work was completed by the deadline
- ❑ Made special efforts to maintain high standards
- ❑ Showed initiative in performing to an excellent standard
- ❑ Put job performance above personal considerations

- ❑ Excelled in being prepared and on time to meetings
- ❑ Started work punctually at _____ a.m./p.m.
- ❑ Had high performance in attendance and punctuality
- ❑ Exceeded all company standards of performance and conduct
- ❑ Was a great role model for punctual arrival and meeting preparation
- ❑ Took initiative consistently in making sure subordinates kept time commitments
- ❑ Demonstrated eagerness to see a job through even after normal working hours
- ❑ Did not ever leave work undone
- ❑ Was always on hand when an emergency deadline needed to be met
- ❑ Completed all work assignments completely and on time
- ❑ Set realistic time frames for meetings, etc. and did not fail to meet them
- ❑ Completed all inquiries and requests on his promised schedule
- ❑ Finished assignments by the deadline with high accuracy
- ❑ Maintained excellent attendance and punctuality standards for subordinates
- ❑ Began and ended meetings on time
- ❑ Created a positive work environment by punctually and completely responding to requests
- ❑ Had a perfect on-time attendance record
- ❑ Arranged for backup and temporary support whenever needed
- ❑ Performed beyond expectations on a regular basis
- ❑ Orchestrated timetables to maximize productivity
- ❑ Was always prepared to start work on time

❹ Exceeded Standards (ES)

- ❑ Arrived at work on time and prepared to start work ____% of the time
- ❑ Showed good performance on preparation for meetings

- ❑ Made special efforts often to coordinate with interrelated departments to facilitate seamless production and avoid downtime
- ❑ Performed well above average consistently
- ❑ Arranged for backup ____% of the time
- ❑ Had very good attendance at interdepartmental meetings
- ❑ Complied with organization requirements and standards, and sometimes initiated improvements
- ❑ Maintained client satisfaction levels at ____% to ____%
- ❑ Had an attendance record at after-hours meetings of ____%
- ❑ Did not fail to show up when an overtime emergency occurred
- ❑ Avoided department downtime with careful scheduling on ____ occasions
- ❑ Stayed in touch with subordinates most of the workday

❸ Met Standards (MS)

- ❑ Arrived on time and prepared to start work ____% to ____% of the time
- ❑ Met requirements for production, but didn't exceed them
- ❑ Got department working within ____ minutes of her arrival
- ❑ Demonstrated good attendance for periods of time and then was tardy several days in a row
- ❑ Obtained prior approval for being absent ____% of the time
- ❑ Remained at his workstation during work hours approximately ____% of the time
- ❑ Arrived at meetings on time ____% of the time
- ❑ Demonstrated that she was prepared and ready for meetings ____% to ____% of the time
- ❑ Completed assignments on time and with high accuracy ____% to ____% of the time
- ❑ Adhered to deadlines ____% of the time

❷ Below Standards (BS)

- ❑ Met the standard for on-time arrival and preparedness to start work ____% of the time

- ❑ Failed to follow proper protocol for call-ins for absence ____% of the time

- ❑ Arrived late for meetings ____% of the time and didn't demonstrate the proper preparation

- ❑ Demonstrated disorganization in handling the start and progression of meetings

- ❑ Allowed personal interruptions by telephone calls during meetings ____% of the time

- ❑ Was absent from his workstation approximately ____% of the time

- ❑ Showed a casual attitude toward meeting interdepartmental time schedules to ensure work production and eliminate down time

- ❑ Set a poor example for subordinates about the importance of following written procedures and regulations

- ❑ Failed to arrange backup coverage when absent about ____% of the time

- ❑ Was often not available for after-hours emergencies

- ❑ Used all sick and personal days allowed, plus ____ additional days

- ❑ Was absent without approval or notifying his department ____ times

❶ Far Below Standards (FBS)

- ❑ Arrived late for work ____% to ____% of the time

- ❑ Failed to notify superior when she was going to be absent

- ❑ Did not follow rules and regulations for attendance ____% to ____% of the time

- ❑ Was absent from his workstation over ____% of the time

- ❑ Had sporadic attendance at meetings and often arrived unprepared to participate

- ❑ Demonstrated little respect for the time of others in coordinating interdepartmental activities

- ❑ Used ____ more than his allotted sick and personal leave days
- ❑ Spent time on the Internet for personal use on an average of ____ hour(s) each workday
- ❑ Left department unreachable ____% of the time during work hours
- ❑ Was not available for after-hours special meetings or emergencies ____% of the time
- ❑ Delivered work late ____% of the time and had production waste factor of ____% above the acceptable level
- ❑ Caused work stoppage ____ times due to production errors
- ❑ Had an overall performance rate of ____% below expectations
- ❑ Accrued an unacceptable attendance and punctuality record of

  _____

❶ Not Observed (NO), Not Ratable (NR), Not Applicable (NA), Failed (F)

- ❑ No records exist to measure his punctuality because of his exempt status
- ❑ Arrived late to work ____ times
- ❑ Did not attend department management-level meetings
- ❑ Customer input and rating reports do not exist
- ❑ Was not responsible for department work-start time
- ❑ Failed to show up at work, or call in, resulting in termination
- ❑ Was too new to be rated
- ❑ Job does not require interdepartmental coordination
- ❑ Interdepartmental assessment report does not exist
- ❑ Exempt status does not require rating
- ❑ Failed to make it to ____ departmental meetings
- ❑ Was unprepared for meetings over ____% of the time

Recommended Action Steps for the Manager

- Review the positive behavior of the employee.
- Have employee explain his deficiencies and challenges.

- Require that the employee write a plan for how she will start to meet her on-time and start-work requirements, starting immediately.
- Ask the employee to keep a diary of his attendance for the next quarter, and set a date to review it with him each week.

Communication Skills—Verbal

Good communications skills are vital to every job, but this is an area where many employees are woefully lacking. The manager who encourages his subordinates to increase their skills, and helps them with the tools to do so, will reap the rewards in many ways.

❺ Outstanding (O)

- ❑ Delivered powerful and persuasive speech(es)
- ❑ Demonstrated the ability to speak to his audience at their level without talking down
- ❑ Exhibited spokesperson skills at the highest level
- ❑ Self-edited while she spoke and was concise and thorough in her presentation
- ❑ Connected very effectively with his audience, making them enthusiastic listeners
- ❑ Was organized and balanced in PowerPoint presentations; was rated excellent in audience evaluations
- ❑ Showed willingness to ask astute questions in order to completely understand material being presented
- ❑ Demonstrated telephone presentation skills that were extraordinary
- ❑ Was rated at ____% by peers in his ability at departmental meeting presentations
- ❑ Displayed enthusiasm that was infectious

4 Exceeded Standards (ES)

- ❑ Showed conviction and confidence in making presentations
- ❑ Demonstrated telephone presentation skills that were very good
- ❑ Organized presentations so the audience followed easily
- ❑ Summarized well and concluded on upbeat action points
- ❑ Maintained good eye contact and answered questions concisely and completely
- ❑ Presented logical solutions in steps her audience could follow
- ❑ Asked questions until he understood
- ❑ Rated at ____% for efficiency in departmental meeting presentations
- ❑ Generated a good level of enthusiasm in his audience

3 Met Standards (MS)

- ❑ Rated at ____% by audiences for PowerPoint presentations
- ❑ Rated at ____% by his peers for efficiency in departmental meeting presentations
- ❑ Presented logical solutions his audience could follow ____% of the time
- ❑ Demonstrated acceptable telephone presentation skills
- ❑ Closed sales after presentations ____% of the time
- ❑ Digressed ____% of the time during presentations
- ❑ Made occasional grammatical errors during presentations
- ❑ Was sometimes unclear in his presentation of logical progressions when he spoke
- ❑ Needed to demonstrate better elocution skills

2 Below Standards (BS)

- ❑ Spoke with many grammatical errors
- ❑ Lacked eye contact with audience while presenting
- ❑ Let her delivery wander and roam without making concise points

- Failed to elicit audience participation during presentations
- Relied on written notes when speaking
- Lacked enthusiastic spark when speaking; had monotone delivery
- Was unable to self-edit or adapt to be more spontaneous
- Lacked the needed effective-listening skills to perform better
- Relied on others in group discussions
- Failed to ask necessary questions during group discussions

❶ Far Below Standards (FBS)

- Was silent during departmental meetings when he should have been offering answers and asking questions
- Took no leadership role in discussions
- Deferred to others on the team to make presentations
- Did not present well on the telephone or during teleconferences
- Demonstrated a fear of public speaking
- Failed to ask pertinent questions during group discussions
- Did not possess the necessary grammar and elocution skills

⓪ Not Observed (NO), Not Ratable (NR), Not Applicable (NA), Failed (F)

- Had no record of verbal participation during group discussions or departmental meetings, and had no presentations
- Not suited for verbal participation at this time
- Was unable to function in this capacity
- Was not rated
- Received customers rating score of "failed" in presenting skills
- Lost the company ____ accounts due to abusive language used during telephone calls

- Review the suggestions at the end of this section (see page 171) and select those that apply.

- Ask employee to attend in-house sales training classes for the next quarter and then reassess.

- Ask the employee to write his own plan for how he will increase his skill in this area within the next quarter, then meet within the week to assess and approve the plan, and have the employee sign it.

Communication Skills—Written

Employees' lack of written communication skills costs organizations billions of dollars each year. The manager who recognizes, rewards, and fosters outstanding written communication skills in subordinates will see the results in both improved goal attainment for the organization and increased employee development and growth.

⑤ Outstanding (O)

❑ Wrote proposals that resulted in ____% success rate in obtaining new client contracts

❑ Used excellent grammar and punctuation ____% of the time

❑ Possessed a 100% error-free record on all written communications

❑ Wrote bids that resulted in ____ of ____ prospect-to-new-customer conversions

❑ Was effective in writing information in very understandable language

❑ Responded to writing assignments quickly, completely, and effectively

❑ Wrote proposals that were well focused on potential customer needs and wants

❑ Hit the target in summarizing information on reports

❑ Was analytical and concise in presenting information

❹ Exceeded Standards (ES)

- ❏ Wrote proposals that resulted in ____% success rate in obtaining new client contracts
- ❏ Completed reports and proposals with what was usually clear, concise, and effective writing
- ❏ Completed writing assignments in a timely manner
- ❏ Made few typos and grammatical errors in writing assignments
- ❏ Wrote customer bids that resulted in contracts ____ out of ____ times
- ❏ Formatted effectively to emphasize key points
- ❏ Summarized and concluded reports in well-stated and logical manner

❸ Met Standards (MS)

- ❏ Wrote proposals that resulted in obtaining ____ new client contracts— a ____% conversion rate
- ❏ Met acceptable level for report and proposal clarity, conciseness, and writing effectiveness
- ❏ Completed reports and proposals that usually met deadlines
- ❏ Committed grammatical errors and typos on writing assignments within acceptable limits
- ❏ Completed customer bids that resulted in contracts ____ out of ____ times
- ❏ Performed at acceptable levels in writing reports and stating logical and comprehensive summaries and conclusions

❷ Below Standards (BS)

- ❏ Wrote proposals that resulted in only ____% success rate in obtaining new clients
- ❏ Needed reminders to get reports and proposals in after deadline ____% of the time
- ❏ Did not meet standard for report and proposal clarity, conciseness, and writing effectiveness
- ❏ Wrote bids with only ____% new work success rate

- ❑ Produced writing assignments with unacceptable grammar and typographical errors
- ❑ Recorded summaries and conclusions that did not meet requirements

❶ Far Below Standards (FBS)
- ❑ Wrote proposals that failed to obtain clients ____% of the time
- ❑ Delivered reports and proposals late ____% of the time
- ❑ Failed routinely to meet standard for report and proposal clarity, conciseness, and writing effectiveness
- ❑ Obtained only ____% bid success rate
- ❑ Made unacceptable number of grammatical and typographical errors in writing assignments
- ❑ Reached incorrect conclusions and inadequate summaries ____% of the time

❶ Not Observed (NO), Not Ratable (NR), Not Applicable (NA), Failed (F)
- ❑ Not applicable to this position
- ❑ Not rated
- ❑ Not observed
- ❑ Failed writing requirements

Recommended Action Steps for the Manager

- ■ Review the suggestions at the end of this section (see page 171) and select those that apply.
- ■ Ask the employee to take the initiative to upgrade his writing skills by ____% within the next quarter.
- ■ Insist that the employee set a goal for a ____% improvement in his bid conversion rate.
- ■ Ask the employee to reduce grammatical and typographical errors on reports, proposals, and bids by ____%, as measured by quality control, within the next quarter.

- Suggest that the employee complete a community college basic English or writing program in the next six months.
- Ask the employee to write up a plan that states how he will improve his writing skills and to submit that plan in the next week.

Conceptual Thinking

The ability to focus on the theoretical and think "outside the box" and to come up with new, and perhaps radically different, approaches to overcome constraints is a rare quality. Weight it according to its value for the employee's position.

5 Outstanding (O)

- ❏ Saw the big picture; didn't get lost in the details
- ❏ Applied the theoretical framework to understand the specific situation very effectively
- ❏ Did not overthink problems and was able to quickly isolate and solve individual problem parts
- ❏ Was able to analyze complex problems, divide them into manageable parts, and successfully solve each one in a methodical way
- ❏ Ordered and prioritized skillfully so work got done
- ❏ Constructed procedural graphs and work-flow diagrams quickly and easily
- ❏ Exhibited exceptional skill at grouping like functions together
- ❏ Explained complex concepts and ideas to subordinates by skillfully using analogies and metaphors

4 Exceeded Standards (ES)

- ❏ Grasped the big picture quickly
- ❏ Applied the theoretical framework to understand a specific situation
- ❏ Was able to isolate and solve individual parts of a complex problem ____% of the time
- ❏ Had a good grasp on ordering and prioritizing work to be done

- ❑ Could often graph procedures and diagram work flow to make the processes understandable
- ❑ Grouped like functions together fairly well
- ❑ Explained complex concepts and ideas to subordinates by using analogies and metaphors

❸ Met Standards (MS)

- ❑ Identified specific problems according to the theoretical framework _____% of the time
- ❑ Was able to break down and solve individual problem parts _____% of the time
- ❑ Had a firm grasp on ordering and prioritizing work to be done
- ❑ Could graph procedures and diagram work flow to make procedures understandable with some assistance
- ❑ Isolated and grouped like functions together fairly well
- ❑ Did occasionally explain complex concepts and ideas to subordinates by using analogies and metaphors

❷ Below Standards (BS)

- ❑ Identified specific problems according to the theoretical framework only _____% of the time
- ❑ Broke down and solved problem parts _____% of the time
- ❑ Needed assistance in ordering and prioritizing work to be done _____% of the time
- ❑ Was able to graph procedures and diagram work flow to make procedures understandable only with assistance
- ❑ Was not able to grasp complex concepts and ideas or explain them by using analogies and metaphors

❶ Far Below Standards (FBS)

- ❑ Was unable to identify specific problems and put them in the theoretical framework
- ❑ Was not able to break down and solve problem parts

- ❑ Seemed overwhelmed by the task of prioritizing and ordering work to be done
- ❑ Was inept at diagramming work flow and graphing procedures
- ❑ Did not demonstrate the ability to grasp complex concepts or explain them by using analogies

Not Observed (NO), Not Ratable (NR), Not Applicable (NA), Failed (F)
- ❑ Not applicable to this position
- ❑ Was not able to observe
- ❑ Not ratable
- ❑ Not applicable
- ❑ Failed to demonstrate the necessary abilities and aptitude for this skill

Recommended Action Steps for the Manager

- Ask the employee to agree to a mentorship with a skilled employee to bring his skill levels up by ____% within the next quarter.
- Suggest that the employee enroll in a conceptual-thinking class at a local technical or community college.
- Suggest a self-study program targeting a skill level increase of ____% in the next quarter.
- Ask the employee to participate in an after-hours organization class in critical thinking with a target of a ____% skill increase in the next quarter.

Conflict Management

Certainly not all jobs require this skill, but those with supervisory responsibilities need to be able to spot trouble before it develops and step in before a conflict boils into a problem. Weight this skill with this in mind.

❺ Outstanding (O)

- ❑ Saw approaching trouble before it became a problem and developed a solution
- ❑ Was able to diffuse conflicts ____% of the time
- ❑ Subdued escalation of conflicts by encouraging subordinates to come up with solutions and commit to them
- ❑ Did not tolerate negativity in his department
- ❑ Converted adversaries to amenable team members and partners ____% of the time
- ❑ Did troubleshooting for problem areas and planned for conflict-avoiding procedures
- ❑ Mediated conflicts between subordinates successfully ____% of the time
- ❑ Was proactive in promoting harmony both among coworkers and with customers

❹ Exceeded Standards (ES)

- ❑ Was able to diffuse conflicts ____% of the time
- ❑ Avoided escalation of conflicts between subordinates, and with clients, by stepping in with solutions ____% of the time
- ❑ Handled conflicts with customers fairly well ____% of the time
- ❑ Was often able to find a place of common agreement
- ❑ Heard all sides of a conflict before suggesting solutions
- ❑ Negotiated compromise quite skillfully
- ❑ Remained composed and calm in the face of escalating conflict
- ❑ Used diplomacy effectively

❸ Met Standards (MS)

- ❑ Employed the proper mediation techniques to resolve conflicts
- ❑ Asked for assistance when conflicts escalated
- ❑ Remained calm and collected in ____% of conflict situations
- ❑ Served effectively as intermediary when asked by other departments

- ❑ Was able to evaluate when outside help was needed, and sought it
- ❑ Exercised restraint and didn't jump into conflicts prematurely

❷ Below Standards (BS)

- ❑ Showed impatience with those in a dispute
- ❑ Demonstrated a lack of ability to remain objective in subordinate conflicts
- ❑ Let trouble brew when stepping in could have effectively nipped a problem in the bud
- ❑ Showed passivity rather than conflict resolution
- ❑ Blamed others when a conflict grew
- ❑ Failed to ask for help when needed

❶ Far Below Standards (FBS)

- ❑ Refused to reach a compromise
- ❑ Displayed negative attitude, which promoted conflict among subordinates and coworkers
- ❑ Took sides during conflicts and became embroiled in them
- ❑ Lost objectivity completely during a conflict
- ❑ Failed to follow conflict resolution procedures or ask for help
- ❑ Inflamed conflicts by insisting on getting his way

❶ Not Observed (NO), Not Ratable (NR), Not Applicable (NA), Failed (F)

- ❑ Not a skill required for this position
- ❑ Not observed
- ❑ Not applicable
- ❑ Not ratable
- ❑ Failed to meet the most minimal requirement of conflict resolution

Recommended Action Steps for the Manager

- ▪ Review the suggestions at the end of this section (see page 171) and select those that apply.
- ▪ Prescribe tutoring by HR personnel for this employee.

- Arrange a mentorship with an employee who possesses outstanding conflict management skills.
- Suggest an in-service or online class in conflict resolution.
- Present to the employee possible online or community classes in conflict resolution in which she might consider enrolling.
- Ask the employee to formulate a plan and make a commitment to improve this skill by ____% in the next quarter, and then make a schedule to review progress with the employee.

Cooperation

Essential to any position within an organization is the personal skill of being cooperative and willing to work with others on the team—a willingness to combine good efforts to produce the best outcome. This skill should be weighted more heavily, of course, for positions where the operation of other departments and management of employees is accelerated by the positive attitude, willingness, and helpfulness of the employee.

❺ Outstanding (O)
- ❏ Looked for ways to help others and work together
- ❏ Promoted teamwork in everything he did
- ❏ Consulted with all others who were affected by decisions to get their input and keep them fully informed, while making sure the process kept moving forward
- ❏ Exhibited concern for others in decision making ____% of the time
- ❏ Could be depended on to be forthright and honest with coworkers
- ❏ Led teams in a manner that encouraged contributions from all members
- ❏ Pitched in to help when needed
- ❏ Was receptive to working with anyone on the team
- ❏ Built consensus

- ❏ Gained the respect and cooperation of others
- ❏ Promoted team spirit above individual recognition
- ❏ Showed great ability to resolve conflicts without alienating others
- ❏ Raised the level of positive energy and production of the team

④ Exceeded Standards (ES)

- ❏ Showed a good ability to help others and promoted working together ____% of the time
- ❏ Elicited input from other team members ____% of the time
- ❏ Exhibited a high level of concern for others in decision making
- ❏ Was usually forthright and honest with coworkers
- ❏ Led teams focusing on encouraging all members to contribute ____% of the time
- ❏ Gained the respect and cooperation of others ____% of the time
- ❏ Promoted team spirit above individual recognition ____% of the time
- ❏ Showed good ability to resolve conflicts without alienating others

❸ Met Standards (MS)

- ❏ Demonstrated ability to help others and promote working together ____% of the time
- ❏ Solicited input from other team members ____% of the time
- ❏ Exhibited concern for others in decision making ____% of the time
- ❏ Encouraged all team members to contribute ____% of the time
- ❏ Gained the respect and cooperation of others ____% of the time
- ❏ Used effective diplomacy ____% of the time
- ❏ Promoted team spirit occasionally
- ❏ Could sometimes resolve team conflicts without assistance and without alienating others

❷ Below Standards (BS)

- ❏ Did not demonstrate the necessary ability to help others and promote working together
- ❏ Was not able to gain the input and cooperation of others on the team

- ❏ Failed to promote team member contributions
- ❏ Promoted personal achievements at the expense of the team
- ❏ Made decisions without team member input or consideration
- ❏ Did not gain the respect and cooperation of team members
- ❏ Was unable to effectively resolve team conflicts without outside intervention; alienated others

❶ Far Below Standards (FBS)

- ❏ Alienated coworkers and subordinates
- ❏ Refused to relate to coworkers and subordinates
- ❏ Used a completely arbitrary style, making decisions for others
- ❏ Had ____ complaints from coworkers and subordinates in the review period for failure to be a team player
- ❏ Demonstrated a complete disconnect with coworkers and subordinates
- ❏ Was so impatient with team members that they refused to work with him
- ❏ Required intervention from HR ____ times during the review period

❶ Not Observed (NO), Not Ratable (NR), Not Applicable (NA), Failed (F)

- ❏ Not applicable
- ❏ Is not suited for this role
- ❏ Failed to meet the criteria
- ❏ Not ratable
- ❏ Not observed

Recommended Action Steps for the Manager

- ■ See suggestions at the end of this section (page 171) and include all those that apply.
- ■ Ask the employee to create a set of goals for how he will improve his cooperation in the next quarter, and arrange meetings to review and adjust those goals each week.

Creativity

The importance of this skill is magnified in jobs like copywriting, advertising, and marketing, but it is also an invaluable organizational asset in many other areas. Weight it to reward the employee's role for it in the organization.

❺ Outstanding (O)

- ❏ Brought fresh and new ideas to each project
- ❏ Thought outside the box when faced with challenges
- ❏ Questioned old routines and practices in order to create more efficient ones
- ❏ Came up with unique, workable, and energizing ideas and concepts for old practices
- ❏ Was able to think about procedures in a new way
- ❏ Developed marketing concepts that won ____ new clients in the last year
- ❏ Reduced time spent on projects by ____% by designing new review and sign-off procedures
- ❏ Created new sales approach that increased sales last quarter by ____%
- ❏ Promoted creativity within the department by using creative brainstorming sessions
- ❏ Encouraged creativity in subordinates and embraced new ideas
- ❏ Instituted bonus system that rewarded creativity among subordinates
- ❏ Offered creative solutions ____% of the time

❹ Exceeded Standards (ES)

- ❏ Was often able to bring a new and fresh approach to projects
- ❏ Offered a unique and workable idea for failing practices

- Was consistently able to think about old procedures in a new way to solve problems
- Used good creative marketing skills
- Fine-tuned old procedures to reduce labor
- Created new approach to sales pitches that increased sales last quarter by ____%
- Recognized creative, workable ideas from subordinates and was willing to implement them
- Offered creative solutions ____% of the time

❸ Met Standards (MS)

- Offered occasionally creative solutions and ideas to reinvigorate old practices
- Was open to considering new ways of doing things
- Originated new solutions ____% of the time
- Fostered creative contributions from subordinates
- Generated new ideas when old ones were failing
- Created opportunities for his subordinates
- Managed new ideas at an acceptable level

❷ Below Standards (BS)

- Stuck closely to the tried-and-true, old procedures
- Refused to try new ideas until proven
- Depended on others for creativity
- Turned down new ideas presented by subordinates ____% of the time
- Failed to present new ideas to clients most of the time
- Lacked imagination
- Was reluctant to venture into new territory
- Failed to stimulate new ideas from subordinates

❶ Far Below Standards (FBS)

- ❑ Lacked the creativity required by the job description
- ❑ Failed to develop creative ideas presented by subordinates
- ❑ Was unable to imagine possible new procedures and how they could work
- ❑ Brought no new ideas to old problems
- ❑ Suggested others come up with new ideas and refine them before he was willing to try
- ❑ Had client complaints about lack of new and fresh approaches
- ❑ Exhibited criticism of new ideas submitted by others
- ❑ Locked into a set routine, even when it wasn't working
- ❑ Did not submit one new idea in the review period
- ❑ Stymied creativity in subordinates

⓿ Not Observed (NO), Not Ratable (NR), Not Applicable (NA), Failed (F)

- ❑ Not applicable
- ❑ Not observed
- ❑ Lacked completely the aptitude for this job
- ❑ Failed
- ❑ Showed no ability to be creative in the face of failing procedures

Recommended Action Steps for the Manager

- Review the suggestions at the end of the section (see page 171) and include any that are applicable.
- Assign the employee to participate in a planning committee for the next six months.
- Ask the employee to take a creative-thinking course from the local community college, or from an online source.
- Create interdepartmental think tank or brainstorming sessions.
- Ask the employee to come up with a new approach to three problems within the department in the next quarter.

Customer Relations and Service

The final measure of the success of any business is whether the customer is satisfied. While most employees do not have direct contact with customers, it is the business of every manager to raise the consciousness of his subordinates to think in terms of, and consider, the customer first and foremost. Weight this skill most heavily for those employees who deal directly with customers.

❺ Outstanding (O)

- ❏ Focused on what customers want
- ❏ Exhibited empathy for customers and meeting their needs
- ❏ Rated "excellent" by customers in evaluations
- ❏ Used every means possible to solve customer problems
- ❏ Did not have one negative customer evaluation
- ❏ Enjoyed 100% customer loyalty
- ❏ Anticipated customer desires and problems and kept relationships very positive
- ❏ Responded quickly to customer calls and requests
- ❏ Retained his composure with difficult customers
- ❏ Kept customers informed of any changes in products, delivery, or procedures
- ❏ Helped other employees meet their customers' requests

❹ Exceeded Standards (ES)

- ❏ Worked to keep customers loyal to the organization, even in the face of problems
- ❏ Was not rattled or angered when customers were difficult
- ❏ Kept a positive and service-oriented attitude in dealing with customers ____% of the time
- ❏ Found ways to meet even some exceptional or unreasonable customer demands
- ❏ Remained calm and collected in the face of angry customers

- Promoted good customer relations and service among other employees
- Conducted herself in a professional manner at all times
- Went the extra mile in educating customers to win loyalty
- Made personal sacrifices to be sure customer commitments were met

❸ Met Standards (MS)

- Represented the organization well
- Displayed courtesy and product knowledge when customers asked
- Met the requirements for professional conduct
- Created solutions when customers were unhappy
- Was usually able to solve routine customer problems
- Asked for assistance for exceptional customer dissatisfaction situations
- Maintained professional appearance and protocol

❷ Below Standards (BS)

- Showed impatience with customers ____% of the time
- Showed a lack of care in maintaining professional appearance and protocol
- Needed assistance with routine customer problems
- Took few proactive steps to meet customer needs and requests
- Followed up on customer complaints and requests only ____% of the time
- Lacked product and procedure knowledge required to do his job well
- Possessed little enthusiasm or interest in relating to customers
- Spent over ____% of his time conducting personal business during work hours instead of attending to customers problems

❶ Far Below Standards (FBS)

- ❑ Received ____ customer complaints rating him "rude"
- ❑ Dropped the ball on following up on customer requests and complaints
- ❑ Showed impatience with elderly customers
- ❑ Was inflexible in making customer accommodations
- ❑ Failed to listen to customer complaints
- ❑ Completed the customer forms incorrectly
- ❑ Presented unprofessional appearance
- ❑ Received ____ customer complaints rating their experience with him unacceptable

⓪ Not Observed (NO), Not Ratable (NR), Not Applicable (NA), Failed (F)

- ❑ Not applicable
- ❑ Not ratable
- ❑ Failed to meet the essential customer relations requirements
- ❑ Did not pass the product knowledge test
- ❑ Was unable to function in this role

Recommended Action Steps for the Manager

- ▪ Review the suggestions at the end of this section (see page 171) and select all that are appropriate.
- ▪ Ask the employee to take the product-training course again.
- ▪ Insist that the employee commit to improving his customer-relations skills through role playing with an organization mentor.
- ▪ Enroll the employee in the sales training program again.
- ▪ Ask the employee to agree to a mentorship with an outstanding customer service employee.
- ▪ Set a goal of increasing the employee's customer service ratings by ____% in the next quarter.

- Restrict personal business during work hours to breaks and lunchtime.

- Require the employee to attend the professional appearance employee training class.

- Ask the employee to write up a plan for how she will improve her skills within the next quarter and meet within the next week to review and approve progress on meeting the plan.

Decision-Making Skills

Every employee must make some decisions in the course of doing his job, even if the decision is whether to defer to someone else. Weight this skill consistent with the employee's decision-making scope and the impact his decisions have on customers, other employees, and the organization.

❺ Outstanding (O)

- ❑ Weighed all the pertinent options and risks carefully before making a decision

- ❑ Was able to project his thinking into the consequences of decisions and make effective ones ____% of the time

- ❑ Gathered all the necessary facts and complete information and got input from others affected before making decisions

- ❑ Was thorough in following procedures for making decisions ____% of the time

- ❑ Made difficult decisions expediently

- ❑ Could be counted on to make difficult decisions in a timely, effective manner

- ❑ Took responsibility—did not defer to others, procrastinate, or pass the buck

- ❑ Made tough decisions with ease

- ❑ Communicated decisions with confidence

- ❑ Supported his decisions with rationale and facts

❹ Exceeded Standards (ES)

- ❏ Demonstrated leadership in making decisions others shrank from making
- ❏ Avoided hasty decisions
- ❏ Assembled all the pertinent data and consulted with others most of the time before making decisions
- ❏ Weighed theoretical and practical consequences before making decisions
- ❏ Owned a track record of making correct decisions ____% of the time
- ❏ Considered all approaches before making decisions
- ❏ Modeled outcomes carefully before making decisions
- ❏ Was willing to make decisions that might be unpopular
- ❏ Communicated decision rationale effectively and confidently

❸ Met Standards (MS)

- ❏ Owned a track record of making ____% expedient decisions
- ❏ Was usually able to be decisive
- ❏ Consulted with others and preferred to make decisions in concert
- ❏ Delayed decision making until others were onboard with it
- ❏ Sought staff input before arriving at a decision ____% of the time
- ❏ Demonstrated good skills at modeling possible outcomes
- ❏ Gathered most of the pertinent information before making decisions

❷ Below Standards (BS)

- ❏ Needed assistance and considerable hand-holding and consensus before making a decision
- ❏ Often deferred to others to make the final decision
- ❏ Displayed weak skills in modeling possible outcomes of decisions
- ❏ Failed to collect all the necessary facts and information before starting the decision-making process
- ❏ Delayed making necessary decisions
- ❏ Avoided making decisions whenever possible

- ❏ Waffled on taking responsibility for decisions
- ❏ Did not possess the needed analytical skills that should proceed the decision step

❶ Far Below Standards (FBS)

- ❏ Paralyzed by fear of making the wrong decision
- ❏ Did not anticipate problems in advance
- ❏ Made decisions only when forced into it
- ❏ Failed to apply the needed logic in decision making
- ❏ Refused to make decisions
- ❏ Made the wrong decision ____% of the time
- ❏ Failed to perform due diligence before making a decision

⓪ Not Observed (NO), Not Ratable (NR), Not Applicable (NA), Failed (F)

- ❏ Not observed
- ❏ Not required in this position
- ❏ Not ratable
- ❏ Failed to make all necessary decisions required by the job
- ❏ Demonstrated complete inability to function in this capacity

Recommended Action Steps for the Manager

- Review the suggestions at the end of this section (see page 171) and adapt and include any that are appropriate.
- Promote a mentorship with another employee who excels in decision making.
- Ask the employee to enroll in appropriate community college classes or online courses to raise his skill level by ____% in the next quarter.
- Ask the employee to reassess his desire to do this job and decide if he's willing to upgrade his decision-making skills.

- Ask the employee to commit to interview leading organization decision makers and employ their advice about upgrading her skill level in the next quarter.
- Require the employee to write up a plan within the week for how he will improve his skill level and schedule a meeting time to review and approve the plan or make adjustments.

Delegating

The efficient employee with supervisory responsibilities must be able to decide what he can accomplish best by assigning tasks to others. Not every employee needs this skill, but when it's necessary to the efficient function of the job, it must be weighted heavily.

❺ Outstanding (O)

- ❏ Matched assigned tasks to subordinates very well
- ❏ Oversaw assigned tasks to eliminate errors 100% of the time
- ❏ Strengthened department output by ____% through effective delegating
- ❏ Offered great support to delegates by connecting them to expert sources
- ❏ Increased subordinates' skills through making challenging assignments
- ❏ Followed through on assignments in an excellent fashion
- ❏ Expanded department scope through careful delegation
- ❏ Employed a very effective system of delegating
- ❏ Trained subordinates thoroughly and tested their skills before delegating to them
- ❏ Had increased quality and production and reduced errors through effective delegating
- ❏ Helped ____ subordinates gain new skill levels to take on new responsibilities

- ❑ Followed up on all delegated assignments to ensure quality and production
- ❑ Designed system of delegated responsibilities to ensure coverage in all situations

❹ Exceeded Standards (ES)

- ❑ Matched most tasks to subordinates well
- ❑ Oversaw assigned tasks to eliminate errors ____% of the time
- ❑ Kept subordinates enthusiastic with new and challenging assignments
- ❑ Allowed subordinates latitude to try new areas
- ❑ Assigned tasks to subordinates who demonstrated aptitude and some skill
- ❑ Demonstrated good assessment of skill levels before new task assignment
- ❑ Used delegation often to increase subordinates' job satisfaction
- ❑ Kept tabs on delegated projects most of the time
- ❑ Instituted training programs for subordinates to help them increase their skill levels and career development
- ❑ Did not interfere with delegated projects
- ❑ Trained subordinates properly before giving them assignments
- ❑ Gave subordinates the authority to complete and manage assigned projects

❸ Met Standards (MS)

- ❑ Made assignments when workload became heavy
- ❑ Managed assignees adequately; few complaints from subordinates
- ❑ Delegated routine tasks to subordinates with proven skills
- ❑ Tried to balance assigned tasks between mundane and challenging
- ❑ Used the fairness standard to delegate between subordinates
- ❑ Kept subordinates' assignments and workloads manageable most of the time

- Gave subordinates the necessary resources to complete assignments most of the time
- Delegated fairly between subordinates
- Checked on assignment progress routinely most of the time
- Trained subordinates before making assignments ____% of the time
- Balanced assignments for subordinates between challenging and routine

❷ Below Standards (BS)

- Needed to perform better oversight of assigned tasks
- Showed reluctance to assign challenging tasks
- Intervened and meddled after assignments were made
- Failed to give clear instructions and support for assignments
- Interfered with progress of assignments by oversupervising
- Made abrupt and frequent changes to assignments due to lack of careful planning
- Failed to check on assigned work ____% of the time
- Kept the challenging assignments for himself most of the time
- Did not offer enough training or background information before making assignments
- Jumped back into projects after making assignments, thus undermining assignees' authority
- Did not assign projects in a timely manner
- Failed to give clear directions or goals in making assignments

❶ Far Below Standards (FBS)

- Failed to delegate as described in his job description
- Missed deadlines ____% of the time due to failure to delegate
- Stockpiled all complex projects for himself
- Demonstrated work quality that suffered due to failure to delegate
- Delegated only when he had not met deadlines, setting assignees up for failure

- ❏ Made assignments with very few or no instructions or support
- ❏ Misassigned projects to subordinates without skills to complete them
- ❏ Refused to delegate even routine tasks
- ❏ Lacked proper knowledge of subordinates' skill levels
- ❏ Did not supply the necessary resources and authority to subordinates given assignments
- ❏ Assigned projects inappropriately
- ❏ Failed to meet goals because of lack of delegation
- ❏ Had not trained employees to take on any of the department's new assignments

Ⓞ Not Observed (NO), Not Ratable (NR), Not Applicable (NA), Failed (F)

- ❏ Not applicable
- ❏ Demonstrates no aptitude for this role
- ❏ Failed to delegate
- ❏ Not observed

Recommended Action Steps for the Manager

- ▪ Review the suggestions at the end of this section (see page 171), and adapt and use those that apply.
- ▪ Ask the employee to analyze subordinates' skills and aptitude for future assignments.
- ▪ Instruct the employee to query subordinates about their project interests.
- ▪ Instruct the employee to increase the number of projects delegated in the next three months by ____%.
- ▪ Have the employee list upcoming projects that may be delegated.
- ▪ Assign the employee to prepare subordinates for projects through training.
- ▪ Have the employee write up a plan for how she will effectively delegate.

- Ask the employee if he is willing to commit to being mentored by an employee with excellent delegating skills with the goal of increasing effective delegating by ____% in the next quarter.
- Recommend that the employee transfer to another job.

Dependability

Great job performance and dependability are inseparable when describing a valuable employee. This quality is essential to the efficient operation of every organization.

❺ Outstanding (O)
- ❑ Could always be depended on to deliver as promised
- ❑ Took complete responsibility for own work
- ❑ Never let coworkers down
- ❑ Took total responsibility for department's quality production
- ❑ Delivered exactly as promised
- ❑ Completed all job requirements without supervision or reminders
- ❑ Possessed a perfect employee record
- ❑ Performed assignments on time and with ____% accuracy
- ❑ Supported coworkers and worked behind the scene to make sure quality was maintained
- ❑ Worked diligently to keep coworker morale high

❹ Exceeded Standards (ES)
- ❑ Delivered as promised ____% of the time
- ❑ Took responsibility for own work
- ❑ Worked hard to not let coworkers down
- ❑ Completed most job requirements without supervision or reminders
- ❑ Showed nearly perfect employee records for punctuality and attendance
- ❑ Achieved a ____% accuracy rate in work assignments

- ❏ Had a good record for boosting coworkers morale
- ❏ Pitched in to help coworkers finish tasks to meet deadlines

❸ Met Standards (MS)

- ❏ Met acceptable standard of accountability for work
- ❏ Delivered on deadline ____% of the time
- ❏ Contributed consistently to department's total effort
- ❏ Achieved a ____% accuracy rate in work assignments
- ❏ Helped to build department morale
- ❏ Pitched in to help coworkers finish tasks to meet deadlines ____% of the time

❷ Below Standards (BS)

- ❏ Registered below acceptable level on delivering his work error free by ____%
- ❏ Delivered work late ____% of the time
- ❏ Needed the help of others to achieve a satisfactory accuracy rate of ____%
- ❏ Underachieved in attendance and punctuality by ____%
- ❏ Was a drain on the department morale

❶ Far Below Standards (FBS)

- ❏ Excused himself on issues of accountability for his work ____% of the time
- ❏ Racked up ____ corrective action marks for deficiencies in punctuality, attendance, department meeting attendance, and employee conduct
- ❏ Did not meet deadlines ____% of the time
- ❏ Failed to appear for special assignments ____ out of ____ times
- ❏ Did not meet ____ of ____ goals
- ❏ Needed constant assistance from supervisors to complete routine work

O **Not Observed (NO), Not Ratable (NR), Not Applicable (NA), Failed (F)**

❏ Not observed

❏ Failed to meet position dependability requirements

Recommended Action Steps for the Manager

- Review the suggestions at the end of this section (see page 171), and adapt any that apply.

- Discuss exact issues of deficiency to find out why the employee is missing the mark and address these.

- Use solid goals for achievement to meet during the next quarter, have the employee list them explicitly, agree to meet them, and sign a personal contract.

Development of Subordinates

The employee who is tasked with developing his subordinates and does it well is very valuable to the organization. Weight this to reflect the portion of the employee's job it represents.

5 **Outstanding (O)**

❏ Was dedicated to staff development and actively looked for new methods of increasing staff growth

❏ Promoted ＿＿＿ staff members after conducting training programs

❏ Found training programs and helped inspire subordinates to enroll and excel

❏ Inspired and motivated subordinates to participate in training

❏ Conducted ＿＿＿ programs of on-the-job training to develop subordinates' new skills

❏ Was an excellent role model for subordinates

❏ Recognized motivated subordinates and accelerated their training

❹ Exceeded Standards (ES)

- ❑ Promoted career development and growth among subordinates
- ❑ Promoted ____ of ____ subordinates in the past year
- ❑ Rated with a score of ____ by subordinates on the development scale
- ❑ Was approachable but still maintained supervisor relationship with subordinates
- ❑ Supported and reinforced new employee programs
- ❑ Made assignments to aid development among subordinates

❸ Met Standards (MS)

- ❑ Gave subordinates new assignments after they completed training
- ❑ Made subordinates aware of in-service training available
- ❑ Scheduled appropriate in-house training regularly
- ❑ Promoted ____ of ____ subordinates in the past year
- ❑ Was rated with a score of ____ by subordinates on the development scale

❷ Below Standards (BS)

- ❑ Did not institute training in a timely manner to help employees develop as quickly as possible
- ❑ Took a piecemeal approach to training, and coverage was not thorough
- ❑ Delivered inadequate training for new subordinates, resulting in their inability to perform to quality standards
- ❑ Did not allow for new techniques training
- ❑ Produced department errors ____% over acceptable rate due to lack of subordinate training

❶ Far Below Standards (FBS)

- ❑ Did not properly train subordinates
- ❑ Frustrated motivated subordinates by failing to give them challenging assignments
- ❑ Left subordinates on their own without adequate training

❑ Failed to promote any subordinate during the review period

❑ Did not conduct orientation for new subordinates

⓪ Not Observed (NO), Not Ratable (NR), Not Applicable (NA), Failed (F)

❑ Had no development responsibilities

❑ Not Ratable

❑ Not observed

❑ Received a poor rating by subordinates for training

❑ Failed to develop subordinates

Recommended Action Steps for the Manager

- Survey employee's subordinates with him to learn how, specifically, training is failing.

- Insist that the employee ask subordinates for ideas on training they would like to have.

- Have the employee study work output records to learn how and where training needs to be improved.

- Review with the employee the training programs and make changes and upgrades.

- Have the employee write up a schedule that includes ____ training sessions every ____.

- Ask the employee to commit to implementing ____ changes to produce a score of ____ on subordinate evaluations by the end of the next quarter.

- Have the employee create a listing of outside sources of training and development to help motivated subordinates excel.

- Review the suggestions at the end of this section (see page 171), and adapt any that apply.

Equal Opportunity and Diversity

All employees must be accepting of their coworkers to ensure everyone has an equal opportunity to perform at their best. Employees who embrace these practices enrich the fabric of the workplace, raise morale, and avoid possible legal hassles.

❺ Outstanding (O)
- ❏ Excelled at offering equal opportunities to all subordinates
- ❏ Worked hard to ensure that subordinate population reflects that of diverse customer base and whole labor pool and population
- ❏ Supported the organization's diversity mission and outreach initiatives
- ❏ Encouraged contributions from all subordinates
- ❏ Conducted meetings to invite diverse ideas and points of view
- ❏ Treated all coworkers equally
- ❏ Built an environment of openness and respect for diverse ideas and opinions
- ❏ Was accepting and sensitive to all coworkers and subordinates
- ❏ Created a task force to promote EEO (Equal Employment Opportunity) practices

❹ Exceeded Standards (ES)
- ❏ Worked to conduct subordinate interaction without bias
- ❏ Promoted on the basis of demonstrated skill and achievement only
- ❏ Was diligent in maintaining equal pay for equal work among subordinates
- ❏ Embraced diversity as a strategic business initiative
- ❏ Established an open-door policy to hear all subordinate views and complaints
- ❏ Tried to identify labor pools that could supply diverse employee candidates

❑ Treated everyone in the work area equally

❑ Did not tolerate discrimination among subordinates

❸ Met Standards (MS)

❑ Used some diversity-based practices in seeking new employees

❑ Instituted a no-tolerance of discrimination policy in her work area with the help of HR

❑ Based promotion of subordinates on performance

❑ Hired new employees from diverse minority groups with the help of HR

❑ Did not demonstrate bias in interactions with subordinates

❑ Worked well with all coworkers

❑ Supported the values of diversity and EEO (Equal Employment Opportunity)

❷ Below Standards (BS)

❑ Needed to institute new practices of EEO (Equal Employment Opportunity) and diversity within department

❑ Did not have a proportionate representation of minorities among subordinates

❑ Had only white males in supervisory roles in department

❑ Refused to work with women and coworkers from minority groups

❑ Did not institute the organization's new program of creating a task force on diversity

❑ Showed some inequity in pay rates for subordinates

❑ Had insufficient number of minority workers in training programs

❶ Far Below Standards (FBS)

❑ Had ____ complaints of discrimination from subordinates

❑ Did not interview any minority applicants for openings

❑ Had ____ reports from subordinates that he made insensitive comments

❑ Told off-color jokes in department meetings

❏ Promoted and/or supported discrimination among coworkers

❏ Owned a record of inequitable pay rates among subordinates

ⓞ Not Observed (NO), Not Ratable (NR), Not Applicable (NA), Failed (F)

❏ Received ____ complaints of sexist, racist, and/or prejudicial comments

❏ Not ratable

❏ Refused to work with minority coworkers

❏ Failed to promote minority workers who were the most qualified for the positions

❏ Not observed

Recommended Action Steps for the Manager

- Ask the employee to hire women and/or members of defined minority groups for ____ out of the next ____ new hires.

- Have the employee write an EEO (Equal Employment Opportunity) and diversity plan for the department and list incremental steps and dates by which action will be taken.

- Insist that the employee apologize to subordinates for any inappropriate comments in the past, and announce a new policy of zero tolerance of discrimination and unacceptable comments and behavior going forward.

- Enroll the employee in sensitivity training to change improper attitudes and behavior.

- Have the employee meet with HR and study legal requirements for meeting EEO (Equal Employment Opportunity) and diversity guidelines and write a plan for complying.

- Ask the employee to establish a plan to recognize the contributions of all subordinates, and correct any inequities in remuneration.

- Have the employee commit to a plan of equal training for all subordinates and write the plan with dates for achievement.

Ethics

In today's diverse work environment, it can't be assumed that all employees share the same values and ethical standards. Therefore it's best to be proactive and include organizational rules and practices of ethical behavior on the job as part of the new employee training program. Rate the employee's performance carefully.

❺ Outstanding (O)

- ❑ Maintained a perfect record and reputation for being scrupulously honest
- ❑ Emphasized ethical conduct in training programs
- ❑ Put ethical considerations above all considerations, including possible personal consequences, and presented a sterling role model
- ❑ Ensured that he adhered to the strictest code of conduct concerning conflict of interest
- ❑ Evaluated by customers and suppliers as holding the highest standard of integrity
- ❑ Exercised the highest principles of honest and open communications with subordinates
- ❑ Held his department to a high ethical standard
- ❑ Gained new customers and retained old ones through attention to treating them with honesty and integrity

❹ Exceeded Standards (ES)

- ❑ Stressed strict adherence to the organization's code of conduct
- ❑ Stood for doing the right thing regardless of the consequences
- ❑ Held a reputation for fair dealing among customers
- ❑ Emphasized never bending the rules
- ❑ Rated very good in standing up for subordinates' rights
- ❑ Exhibited good adherence to ethics training with subordinates
- ❑ Studied and followed applicable laws and regulations

❸ Met Standards (MS)

- ❑ Held a good record of dealing fairly with customers
- ❑ Encouraged code of ethics among subordinates
- ❑ Did not try to bend the rules, find loopholes, or skirt ethical standards
- ❑ Knew the legal regulations for ethical behavior and followed them
- ❑ Was rated as "fair" by ____% of subordinates
- ❑ Received a "good" rating on fairness from ____% of customers

❷ Below Standards (BS)

- ❑ Bent the rules of ethics to improve production numbers
- ❑ Viewed ethics rules as too strenuous sometimes
- ❑ Found that strict adherence to the law was too confining at times
- ❑ Received "unsatisfactory" rating from ____% of customers on fairness issues
- ❑ Encouraged subordinates to cut ethical corners to improve profits
- ❑ Employed a double standard on matters of ethics for subordinates and himself
- ❑ Rated "unfair" in employee dealings by ____% of subordinates
- ❑ Ignored legal regulations on ____ occasions

❶ Far Below Standards (FBS)

- ❑ Failed to uphold standards of ethics
- ❑ Dealt unfairly with customers ____% of the time
- ❑ Did not behave ethically with customers
- ❑ Had ____ ethics violations
- ❑ Was responsible for legal action brought against the organization
- ❑ Infracted the organization's code of ethics

O **Not Observed (NO), Not Ratable (NR), Not Applicable (NA), Failed (F)**

- ❏ Not ratable
- ❏ Not observed
- ❏ Acted unethically in dealing with subordinates
- ❏ Did not admit a conflict of interest and tried to hide the results
- ❏ Lost ____ customers due to unethical behavior
- ❏ Lied to ____ and cost the organization ____ in lost customers and reputation

Recommended Action Steps for the Manager

- Encourage employee to admit the wrong behavior to those affected, apologize, and announce a commitment to change.
- Ask the employee to make atonement for wrongdoing where necessary, and write a commitment to change and a plan for the future—with precise actions and deadlines—and sign it.
- Insist the employee make a commitment to treat everyone with respect and provide everyone an with an equal opportunity.
- Ask subordinates for input on correcting policies that limit fair treatment and equal opportunities.
- Emphasize that the employee must avoid any perception of favoritism or preferential treatment of subordinates.
- Have the employee commit to begin a program to get to know subordinates and their needs in order to help them excel in their careers and advance within the organization.
- Be sure the employee holds all subordinates to the same high standard of ethical behavior.
- Require that the employee write up a plan for making the necessary changes for the next quarter, schedule a meeting within the next week to review and approve the plan, and have the employee sign the approved plan.

Flexibility

Being able to change directions quickly, seamlessly, and without rancor or major disruption is a valuable skill. Weight it according to the need for it within the employee's job description.

⑤ Outstanding (O)

- ❑ Was always willing to work overtime to get a job done when the need occurred
- ❑ Could be counted on to accept and support necessary changes in policy and procedures; cooperate, and compromise
- ❑ Anticipated situations that called for quick procedural changes and incorporated them promptly
- ❑ Was versatile and able to manage multiple projects at the same time, shifting gears quickly and seamlessly
- ❑ Changed production procedure within ____ hours to eliminate errors
- ❑ Dealt easily with interruptions and navigated obstacles in a professional manner
- ❑ Was willing to consider alternatives that might improve outcomes
- ❑ Handled emergencies effectively

④ Exceeded Standards (ES)

- ❑ Stepped in quickly and easily to fill a gap when coworkers needed help
- ❑ Employed an array of alternate techniques and procedures to keep work on schedule
- ❑ Shifted focus and approach easily
- ❑ Filled in for absences whenever necessary
- ❑ Was able to change priorities when directed by manager

③ Met Standards (MS)

- ❑ Cooperated, compromised, and usually made the necessary changes when directed
- ❑ Reset priorities when required

- ☐ Was able to shift gears and step into a number of tasks with less than ____% loss of production
- ☐ Adjusted to changes in procedures with a minimum of downtime
- ☐ Changed schedules and assignments to meet deadlines
- ☐ Accepted required changes in work assignments from superiors with minimal resistance

❷ Below Standards (BS)

- ☐ Resisted necessary changes in work assignments ____% of the time
- ☐ Needed convincing when directed to make changes
- ☐ Had a record of ____% loss in production when he had to implement procedure change
- ☐ Struggled with resetting priorities, cooperating, and compromising
- ☐ Fought any change, even when evidence showed it was the best course
- ☐ Delayed implementing changes when given a deadline

❶ Far Below Standards (FBS)

- ☐ Demonstrated inflexibility when presented with any change
- ☐ Refused to change until threatened with disciplinary action
- ☐ Was unable to change priorities ____% of the time
- ☐ Was listed inflexible by ____ of ____ subordinates
- ☐ Showed an uncooperative attitude with coworkers in instituting changes
- ☐ Exhibited inflexibility that lost the organization ____ customers

❿ Not Observed (NO), Not Ratable (NR), Not Applicable (NA), Failed (F)

- ☐ Not observed
- ☐ Failed to demonstrate the necessary flexibility for the position
- ☐ Not ratable
- ☐ Not applicable

- Review the suggestions at the end of this section (see page 171), and adapt them to help the employee with flexibility.

- Have the employee write a plan for himself that outlines specific areas where he can improve his flexibility, outline the steps he will take to accomplish this, and then commit to making those changes in the next quarter.

- Ask the employee to agree to taking on new areas of responsibility or tasks and sign a personal contract to do so.

Forward Thinking

The employee who is able to project ahead and anticipate the needs, attitudes, and reactions of those with whom he must interact can perform at a higher efficiency rate by eliminating the need to repeat the decision-making steps, coordination steps, and reworking of projects. For some positions, this skill should be rated quite high.

❺ Outstanding (O)

- ❑ Anticipated with nearly 100% accuracy how decisions would be received by coworkers, customers, and the public

- ❑ Held a ____% success-rate record for anticipating possible problems with procedural changes and developed contingency plans in advance

- ❑ Followed industry trends and contributed ideas that pushed the envelope

- ❑ Used futuristic thinking and planning to help the organization stay ahead of the curve

- ❑ Projected accurately the possible consequences of decisions

④ Exceeded Standards (ES)

- ❏ Anticipated with ____% accuracy how decisions would be received by coworkers, customers, and the public

- ❏ Held a ____% success-rate record for anticipating possible problems with procedural changes and developed contingency plans in advance

- ❏ Used the input of others and brainstorming sessions designed to help with anticipating possible problems and developing remedies before new procedures were put in place

- ❏ Used industry trends to inform her decision making

- ❏ Tried to stay ahead of the curve by forming task forces to plan for new products and procedures

③ Met Standards (MS)

- ❏ Was helpful to superiors in predicting how changes would be received by coworkers

- ❏ Contributed some valuable input on task forces charged with brainstorming new products and procedures

- ❏ Anticipated with ____% accuracy possible problems with procedural changes and helped to develop contingency plans in advance

- ❏ Responded well when changes needed to be anticipated and procedures planned to minimize disruptions in workflow

② Below Standards (BS)

- ❏ Was unable to anticipate consequences of procedural and policy changes

- ❏ Needed assistance to institute changes after new procedures resulted in unexpected consequences

- ❏ Let change happen without proper planning and struggled with the aftermath

- ❏ Made a minimal contribution to task-force brainstorming

❶ Far Below Standards (FBS)

- ❏ Was surprised and unprepared for consequences of procedural changes
- ❏ Did not contribute to task-force brainstorming activities
- ❏ Failed to keep coworkers and other departments informed about new procedures
- ❏ Had ____ work stoppages due to unanticipated problems after new procedures were put in place
- ❏ Was unable to anticipate problems or institute changes

❶ Not Observed (NO), Not Ratable (NR), Not Applicable (NA), Failed (F)

- ❏ Not applicable
- ❏ Not ratable
- ❏ Not observed
- ❏ Failed to make any contribution to anticipating repercussions of new procedures

---

Recommended Action Steps for the Manager

- Review the suggestions at the end of the section (see page 171) and adapt any that will help the employee increase her skills in this area.
- Establish a program for rewarding the employee who has exemplary skills of anticipation and forward thinking.
- Make sure the employee understands how important this skill is to his chances for promotion and career development.

Goal Setting

An employee needs concrete and tangible career goals that are properly focused on the organization's goals. If he lacks these goals, he is like the driver who has neither a GPS nor a road map. It is the manager's job to help his subordinates remain properly focused on the organization's goals, and then to help each employee set realistic and attainable goals for his contribution. And it is also the manager's role to help his subordinates achieve those goals. Weight this skill according to the demands for the employee's contribution in this area.

❺ Outstanding (O)

- ❑ Was focused and persistent in pursuing organizational and individual goals
- ❑ Was proactive in setting achievable, specific, measurable, relevant, and time-specific goals for himself
- ❑ Inspired subordinates to set and achieve relevant personal goals
- ❑ Maintained goal focus throughout diverse steps and procedures ____% of the time
- ❑ Understood the importance of goal setting in the achievement process, and had a ____% success rate in reaching goals for the past ____
- ❑ Held subordinates to a high standard of meeting their own set and measurable goals
- ❑ Implemented a system of goal setting that included objective methods of measuring and rewarding success
- ❑ Communicated organizational goals to subordinates and translated these into measurable achievements for his department
- ❑ Created performance standards for subordinates
- ❑ Was ____% successful in getting subordinates to reach department goals

❹ Exceeded Standards (ES)

- ❑ Was realistic in setting achievable goals for department
- ❑ Communicated organizational goals to subordinates successfully ____% of the time
- ❑ Implemented performance standards for subordinates

- Was ____% successful in getting subordinates to sign on to goals programs with concrete performance standards
- Convinced ____% of subordinates to set and achieve their own goals in a ____ -month period
- Translated organizational goals into departmental tasks with ____% success
- Did not lose goal focus
- Inspired his subordinates to reach their goals

❸ Met Standards (MS)

- Complied with goals set by superiors ____% of the time
- Adjusted goals as required by superiors
- Implemented changes required to meet organizational goals ____% of the time
- Set realistic goals for his subordinates
- Worked hard to meet assigned goals and was ____% successful
- Changed goals when necessary
- Was successful in setting short- and long-term goals for department

❷ Below Standards (BS)

- Needed to take a more active role in setting goals for department
- Was unable to set goals with the necessary organizational focus without assistance
- Relied on supervisor to communicate goals
- Lacked self direction and initiative in setting goals for herself
- Resisted supervisor's attempts to set goals
- Had trouble translating organizational goals into work procedures
- Failed to break down long-term goals into short-term steps
- Set goals without consideration to specificity and measurability

❶ Far Below Standards (FBS)

- ❏ Demonstrated a disconnect between organizational goals and his work
- ❏ Resisted all attempts to set meaningful goals
- ❏ Could not translate long-term goals into everyday work procedures and deadlines
- ❏ Failed to meet the goals set in conjunction with his supervisor, ____% of the time
- ❏ Did not accept goals set by his supervisor

⓿ Not Observed (NO), Not Ratable (NR), Not Applicable (NA), Failed (F)

- ❏ Failed to set long- or short-term goals as requested
- ❏ Not observed
- ❏ Not applicable
- ❏ Not ratable
- ❏ Reached only ____ of his ____ personal goals

Recommended Action Steps for the Manager

- Review the suggestions at the end of the section (see page 171) and adapt those that are applicable.
- Review organizational long- and short-term goals with the employee and ask her to write personal goals to implement in her job description.
- Require the employee to write a set of goals for himself and his department and/or subordinates for the next quarter, with specific achievements and dates, and sign it.

Industry and Quality Work Habits

Measuring work output or industriousness and demonstrating sterling work habits show that not only can the employee make an exemplary contribution to the achievement of the organization's goals, but he can also set the standard for other employees. This "soft skill" exhibited by one employee can raise the bar for others and inspire them to reach a new level of accomplishment and performance. Weight this skill to reflect the importance of the employee's contribution.

❺ Outstanding (O)
- ❑ Saw every task through to completion
- ❑ Had an internal gauge that did not allow her to do less than her best
- ❑ Took no task shortcuts when it came to quality of work
- ❑ Approached each task with enthusiasm
- ❑ Did not leave work undone
- ❑ Finished every task well before the deadline
- ❑ Assisted others to ensure every part of the job was done to a high standard
- ❑ Insisted that each task be accomplished to the highest standard
- ❑ Paid very close attention to quality and elimination of errors
- ❑ Made sure coordination with coworkers was complete

❹ Exceeded Standards (ES)
- ❑ Saw most tasks through to completion
- ❑ Produced work that met a high quality standard
- ❑ Took shortcuts only when pushed to do so
- ❑ Showed enthusiasm for his job most of the time
- ❑ Went beyond job requirements to help others complete their tasks
- ❑ Did not procrastinate or delay taking on work at hand
- ❑ Had good work ethic
- ❑ Set a good example for coworkers in accomplishing tasks

❸ Met Standards (MS)
- ❑ Completed projects on time ____% of the time
- ❑ Saw tasks through to completion without supervision ____% of the time

- ❑ Met quality control standards ____% of the time
- ❑ Took shortcuts to try to meet deadlines
- ❑ Contributed to a good work environment
- ❑ Helped others complete their tasks occasionally
- ❑ Did not join in on time-wasting activities

❷ Below Standards (BS)

- ❑ Did not complete projects on time ____% of the time
- ❑ Did not meet quality of work standard ____% of the time
- ❑ Worked consistently on projects only with reminders
- ❑ Took shortcuts frequently (____% of the time) to try to meet deadlines
- ❑ Had ____ complaints for bad attitude and conflicts with coworkers
- ❑ Refused to help others in order to meet own work production deadlines
- ❑ Was written up for time-wasting activities on the job ____ times

❶ Far Below Standards (FBS)

- ❑ Did not complete projects on time ____% of the time
- ❑ Failed to meet the minimum quality control standards ____% of the time
- ❑ Needed to be closely supervised to produce the minimum output
- ❑ Could not work independently
- ❑ Delayed starting work until deadline was looming, and then took wasteful shortcuts
- ❑ Evaluated by coworkers as a troublemaker in ____ out of ____ reports
- ❑ Was cited for wasting time ___ times

❿ Not Observed (NO), Not Ratable (NR), Not Applicable (NA), Failed (F)

- ❑ Failed to meet minimum standard
- ❑ Not observed
- ❑ Not ratable
- ❑ Not applicable
- ❑ Must be terminated due to _____

- Review the suggestions at the end of the section (see page 171) and adapt any that will help the employee improve.

- Have the employee write his own plan outlining how he can increase his value to the organization and the team through personal changes in his work habits.

- Institute a bonus program that rewards industry and good work habits, being sure to spell out precisely what these habits are in terms of the work environment.

- Be sure the employee understands how critical excellent work habits are to being promoted; have her write a plan to improve within this quarter, and sign it.

- Use an ongoing program of recognizing outstanding work habits on a monthly basis.

Initiative

Some employees seem to have almost a sixth sense about what needs to be done and when. They are the people who can look at a task or course of action and anticipate what is best done next, and then take the initiative action to make sure it happens effectively. Weight this skill generously when it results in the employee doing an outstanding job.

❺ Outstanding (O)

- ❑ Looked for opportunities to take the reins
- ❑ Took the proper action at the right time every time
- ❑ Negotiated a ____% discount with suppliers, saving the organization $_____ per year
- ❑ Recalibrated the production equipment to reduce waste by ____%
- ❑ Foresaw and averted a production slowdown by locating new suppliers

- ❏ Reworked the flow of reports to enhance communications by ____%
- ❏ Wrote new policy and procedures for office online communications and avoided organization leaks
- ❏ Anticipated problems and proactively solved them before they happened
- ❏ Was self-motivated in setting and meeting personal goals
- ❏ Helped out in areas not his responsibility
- ❏ Communicated effectively to ensure projects were done correctly and on time
- ❏ Took proactive steps to make sure his team met organization objectives
- ❏ Averted a client crisis by effectively communicating delivery schedule changes

❹ Exceeded Standards (ES)

- ❏ Took initiative ____% of the time
- ❏ Averted problems frequently by taking preventive steps
- ❏ Took proactive steps frequently to streamline production
- ❏ Demonstrated good skills of anticipation and initiative
- ❏ Reworked the flow of reports to enhance communications by ____%
- ❏ Negotiated a ____% discount with ____ suppliers
- ❏ Came up with policy change suggestions to avoid employee conflicts
- ❏ Strived to improve the work process

❸ Met Standards (MS)

- ❏ Took initiative ____% of the time
- ❏ Averted problems by taking preventive steps ____% of the time
- ❏ Took proactive steps often to streamline production
- ❏ Demonstrated skills in anticipating needed changes in procedure ____% of the time
- ❏ Handled problem-solving decisions appropriately
- ❏ Preferred acting within written job description, but sometimes took added initiative

- ❏ Showed some risk-taking ability to solve customer problems
- ❏ Took necessary steps to create a backup system for production
- ❏ Initiated interdepartmental communications to avoid duplication
- ❏ Coordinated with other departments at an acceptable level

❷ Below Standards (BS)
- ❏ Showed discomfort in taking initiative
- ❏ Did only prescribed job description
- ❏ Was slow to act when faced with operational decisions
- ❏ Initiated nothing outside standard procedures
- ❏ Made decisions only with approval
- ❏ Did not foresee or take action to avoid problems in meeting delivery schedule _____ times
- ❏ Lacked confidence to initiate new procedures
- ❏ Failed to step up this part of his game to initiate needed changes

❶ Far Below Standards (FBS)
- ❏ Functioned far below job demands for taking initiative
- ❏ Failed to take initiative when a crisis called for action
- ❏ Did not take initiative until required to do so
- ❏ Delayed making the decision to act until it was too late
- ❏ Missed opportunities to avert customer problems because of lack of initiative
- ❏ Waited for procedure failure before acting
- ❏ Called often on the manager for a decision before taking action

❿ Not Observed (NO), Not Ratable (NR), Not Applicable (NA), Failed (F)
- ❏ Not ratable
- ❏ Not observed
- ❏ Needed to be transferred to another department where this skill was not required
- ❏ Was unable to deliver the initiative required

- ❑ Was unable to function at the job description level
- ❑ Consistently failed to take initiative

Recommended Action Steps for the Manager

- Review the suggestions at the end of the section (see page 171) and adapt any that will help the employee improve.

- Be sure the employee understands how valuable taking the initiative is in order for her to be promoted.

- Have the employee write his own plan outlining how he will increase his value to the organization and his team by taking the initiative in key situations, explaining exactly when, where, and how he will do this within this quarter, and sign it.

Innovation

Creating a new way to get to a goal is a quality that can be extremely valuable, particularly in key positions where methods and measures have topped out in their efficiency. Thinking outside the box in coming up with new solutions to problems and devising better ways of doing things can help the organization reach new heights in productivity and efficiency. Weight this skill based on the employee's need for its application.

❺ Outstanding (O)

- ❑ Could be depended upon to head up new methodology and approaches to problems
- ❑ Came up with efficiencies and streamlined procedures without prompting
- ❑ Was always thinking about better ways to do a task
- ❑ Reduced production costs by ____% by eliminating ____ unnecessary steps in the process
- ❑ Increased production by ____% by making ____ production line changes

- Combined ____ departments into ____, which resulted in better communication and subordinates indicating a ____% increase in job satisfaction
- Instituted a new bonus plan, which has resulted in an increase of ____% in subordinates' production and a ____% decrease in errors

❹ Exceeded Standards (ES)

- Brought innovative ideas to the manager regularly without prompting
- Developed a better system to handle customer complaints and follow-up, which resulted in a ____% increase in customer satisfaction
- Was often thinking about improved ways to reach the department's goals
- Instituted a bonus program for subordinates to reward them for innovation that resulted in better production and higher customer and employee satisfaction
- Volunteered to head up searches for new methodologies and approaches to problems

❸ Met Standards (MS)

- Responded when asked to develop a better procedure
- Came up with improved ways to reach the department's goals ____ times
- Developed a new bonus program when assigned the task
- Did an acceptable job heading up a committee to search for new methods and approaches to a production problem
- Served on the interdepartmental committee for procedure review and action

❷ Below Standards (BS)

- Resisted considering new ways to streamline present processes
- Responded to directives to come up with new problem-solving methods only when given a deadline

- ❏ Failed to produce new efficiencies that were suggested and demonstrated by coworkers
- ❏ Failed to accept and implement new innovations when they were presented

❶ Far Below Standards (FBS)

- ❏ Refused to consider new ways to streamline present processes in more efficient ways
- ❏ Did not develop any problem-solving methods, even when asked to do so
- ❏ Stuck to old methodologies, even when new innovations were proven to increase production, employee morale, and reduce waste
- ❏ Stonewalled attempts to introduce new innovations

❿ Not Observed (NO), Not Ratable (NR), Not Applicable (NA), Failed (F)

- ❏ No applicable
- ❏ Not ratable
- ❏ Does not possess the necessary innovation skills to function in this position
- ❏ Failed to innovate as required
- ❏ Needed to be transferred to another position

Recommended Action Steps for the Manager

- ▪ Review the suggestions at the end of the section (see page 171) and adapt any that apply.
- ▪ Create a mentorship for the employee with another employee who excels in this skill and require the employee show a ____% improvement in the next quarter.
- ▪ Have the employee write up a plan outlining how she will increase his innovation skills in exact terms with dates, and sign the agreement to do this.

Interpersonal Skills

The employee everyone wants to work with is the employee who helps create a work environment that is harmonious and productive. Weight this skill higher when there is the need for close working relationships and lots of interaction among employees.

❺ Outstanding (O)

- ❏ Exuded positive attitude and magnetism that opened up those with whom she interacted—customers, suppliers, coworkers, subordinates
- ❏ Selected first for team participation
- ❏ Exhibited the brand of leadership that got cooperation from others
- ❏ Received praise for attitude, contribution, and likeability
- ❏ Resolved conflicts between subordinates and coworkers easily and quickly
- ❏ Maintained excellent interdepartmental relationships
- ❏ Motivated others to do their best
- ❏ Accepted input and suggestions from everyone equally
- ❏ Practiced model diversity and EEO (Equal Employment Opportunity) principles
- ❏ Showed an authentic interest and care for those he worked with

❹ Exceeded Standards (ES)

- ❏ Held a reputation for getting along with everyone
- ❏ Selected first for team participation
- ❏ Showed leadership in many situations
- ❏ Demonstrated an ability to get others to open up
- ❏ Maintained good interdepartmental relationships
- ❏ Was effective in motivating others to produce at a higher level
- ❏ Practiced diversity and EEO (Equal Employment Opportunity) principles consistently
- ❏ Initiated help projects for ____ colleagues who suffered prolonged illness

❸ Met Standards (MS)

- ❏ Used proper language in the workplace—absent of sexual or racist content
- ❏ Had only ____ subordinate complaints registered in the last ____
- ❏ Could usually get subordinates to follow his lead
- ❏ Was effective in settling disputes ____% of the time
- ❏ Met expectations in communicating with subordinates and coworkers
- ❏ Was often one of the first selected as a team member

❷ Below Standards (BS)

- ❏ Had difficulty in getting the support of her subordinates
- ❏ Could only get a minimum number of subordinates to follow his lead
- ❏ Had ____ subordinate complaints registered against him in the last ____
- ❏ Needed to have assistance in settling disputes ____% of the time
- ❏ Was selected last to serve on teams
- ❏ Exhibited deficits in communication skills
- ❏ Was required to take sensitivity training for ____ complaints by subordinates but showed no improvement

❶ Far Below Standards (FBS)

- ❏ Required disciplinary action ____ times for improper language and sexual comments
- ❏ Had unacceptable number (____) of complaints by customers, clients, coworkers, and/or subordinates in the last ____
- ❏ Was not able to function at the minimum level to resolve disputes
- ❏ Contributed to disputes ____ times in the last ____
- ❏ Was unable to communicate properly with subordinates
- ❏ Was rejected by ____ coworkers as a team member

⓪ Not Observed (NO), Not Ratable (NR), Not Applicable (NA), Failed (F)

- ❏ Failed to exhibit the necessary skills to function in this position
- ❏ Not observed
- ❏ Not ratable
- ❏ Needed to be transferred to another position

Recommended Action Steps for the Manager

- ■ Review suggestions at the end of this section (see page 171) and adapt as many as practical to help the employee improve.
- ■ Require the employee to complete sensitivity training classes.
- ■ Present leadership and communication skills classes to employee and explain the need for her to take them.
- ■ Have the employee write a plan for how he will improve in deficit areas over the next quarter, and sign it.

Job Knowledge

The employee who has a broad-based knowledge of all the factors that affect her job, in addition to the actual "hard skills" and knowledge needed to perform it, will be able to achieve a much higher level of accomplishment than she otherwise would; and she will be able to advance quickly. This is an important basis for excelling within any organization, and should be weighted and recognized according to the demonstrated benefit the organization has received.

❺ Outstanding (O)

- ❏ Possessed an in-depth knowledge of the critical issues, well beyond his job responsibilities, that affect the entire organization
- ❏ Had a rare and extensive knowledge base that enabled her to perform above his job description
- ❏ Understood the purposes, objectives, practices, and procedures of the entire department

- ❏ Was able to teach individual skills because of in-depth knowledge of system functions
- ❏ Shared knowledge with others in a way that made their contributions more meaningful
- ❏ Translated product features into customer benefits very effectively
- ❏ Employed self-study to keep abreast of trends affecting her job and the entire industry
- ❏ Was able to effectively apply his knowledge to improve procedures
- ❏ Was a trusted resource of system-wide knowledge
- ❏ Held professional licenses and/or certificates beyond those required by his job description

❹ Exceeded Standards (ES)

- ❏ Understood the critical issues that affect the organization
- ❏ Performed his job well because he understood its impact on the organization's goals
- ❏ Was able to teach individual skills and explain how they fit into the big picture
- ❏ Was effective in demonstrating how product features benefit customers
- ❏ Performed well as an able organization representative because of her extensive knowledge beyond his own job
- ❏ Kept abreast of trends to be able to better understand the organization's mission
- ❏ Was eager to acquire knowledge far above that required by his job

❸ Met Standards (MS)

- ❏ Kept abreast of changing requirements to keep the department compliant
- ❏ Had a fairly good knowledge of how his department's functions must fit with interrelated departments
- ❏ Ran training sessions for subordinates to help them improve their skills, which were rated ____% satisfactory

- ❑ Held the required certificates/licenses for her job description
- ❑ Took the required courses to stay current on new procedures and requirements

② Below Standards (BS)

- ❑ Needed to take courses to update certificate/licenses required by law
- ❑ Did not have a grasp on the interdependence of his department and others
- ❑ Was lax in offering training sessions for subordinates to make sure the department was in compliance with regulations
- ❑ Took no initiative to keep abreast of changes in the industry or profession
- ❑ Did not take courses to stay current on new procedures and requirements needed to function in his job

① Far Below Standards (FBS)

- ❑ Was delinquent in necessary certification/licensing required by law
- ❑ Refused to function in conjunction with interdependent departments
- ❑ Did not offer required training sessions for subordinates to keep them in compliance with regulations
- ❑ Was unaware of industry changes and new procedures and requirements

⓪ Not Observed (NO), Not Ratable (NR), Not Applicable (NA), Failed (F)

- ❑ Failed to meet the requirements for certification/licensing
- ❑ Not observed
- ❑ Not ratable

Recommended Action Steps for the Manager

- ■ Review suggestions at the end of this section (see page 171) and adapt all that apply.

Judgment

The determination or evaluation that often seems intuitive is referred to as judgment. It is almost always combined with the decision-making process but sometimes stands alone as the pronouncement after a process of consideration. It's an invaluable skill to have and should be weighted in accordance with its importance to the role the employee plays.

❺ Outstanding (O)

- ❑ Was depended upon to be a voice of reason and wisdom after he considered all the facts
- ❑ Remained objective and impartial in weighing every alternative
- ❑ Separated out the emotional issues and was able to reach a conclusion based upon facts and anticipated outcomes
- ❑ Was able to keep an analytical mind, detach herself from her own preferences, and be completely impartial
- ❑ Could reduce any situation to its basic components and determine the best solution
- ❑ Displayed excellent intuition

❹ Exceeded Standards (ES)

- ❑ Remained calm and collected when there was a judgment call to be made
- ❑ Was usually the voice of reason and wisdom after he weighed all the facts
- ❑ Could usually remain objective and impartial in weighing alternatives
- ❑ Was open-minded when forming opinions
- ❑ Followed a systematic and disciplined approach during evaluations
- ❑ Evaluated situations without bias
- ❑ Rendered dispassionate and fair judgments

❸ Met Standards (MS)

- ❏ Could often apply customer values to the situation
- ❏ Was usually able to be objective and fair
- ❏ Analyzed alternatives with input from coworkers and subordinates with ____% total satisfaction rate
- ❏ Gathered information and facts from a number of sources before weighing alternatives
- ❏ Exhibited good intuition most of the time
- ❏ Made a practice of weighing possible consequences

❷ Below Standards (BS)

- ❏ Exhibited poor judgment in ____ cases
- ❏ Did not adequately consider all the facts before making her determination
- ❏ Needed to gather more information and get more input from the right sources before making a final determination
- ❏ Received ____ complaints about his judgment of situations from customers
- ❏ Had trouble being objective in making evaluations
- ❏ Was unable to separate himself from his emotions about situations that required dispassion
- ❏ Tended to inappropriately take sides in subordinate situations

❶ Far Below Standards (FBS)

- ❏ Showed a lack of sound judgment in ____ situations
- ❏ Made a determination on partial and incomplete information
- ❏ Showed favoritism and partiality in decisions
- ❏ Failed to complete the necessary research before rendering a judgment
- ❏ Did not obtain and weigh all considerations adequately and as a result cost the organization ____
- ❏ Displayed high emotions inappropriately in rendering his decisions

(0) **Not Observed (NO), Not Ratable (NR), Not Applicable (NA), Failed (F)**

- ❏ Not observed
- ❏ Failed
- ❏ Did not have the necessary judgment to function in this position

---

Recommended Action Steps for the Manager

- Review the actions at the end of the section (see page 171) and adapt those that can help the employee improve in this area.

- Institute a routine, periodic meeting between the employee and yourself (or the manager) to review the judgments reached, the process of reaching them, and their validity.

Leadership

The employee who influences his subordinates and coworkers to work together to accomplish a common goal or objective in a way that makes her efforts more cohesive and coherent is invaluable. When the position calls for this exceptional skill, be sure to reflect that in the weight you assign.

(5) **Outstanding (O)**

- ❏ Inspired subordinates and coworkers to excel
- ❏ Earned the loyalty of his subordinates by setting a sterling example
- ❏ Projected a rare combination of authority, self-confidence, and enthusiasm that was contagious
- ❏ Was never rattled or off balance in difficult situations or crises
- ❏ Possessed the kind of charisma that subordinates admire, which resulted in the department's high performance
- ❏ Commanded the respect and loyalty of his subordinates through his demonstrated high-level leadership
- ❏ Set an excellent example for his coworkers and subordinates 100% of the time

- ❑ Stood steadfast and asserted authority when challenged
- ❑ Motivated subordinates and coworkers to produce at a record-high level
- ❑ Demanded quality from subordinates and got it

❹ Exceeded Standards (ES)

- ❑ Set a good example for coworkers and subordinates
- ❑ Inspired subordinates to a high level of achievement
- ❑ Exhibited self-confidence in making decisions
- ❑ Generated enthusiasm that was contagious
- ❑ Maintained a high profile in the organization and others sought his counsel
- ❑ Faced problems and crises with confidence and composure
- ❑ Was not afraid to make the difficult decisions and made good ones ____% of the time
- ❑ Got the loyalty of his subordinates ____% of the time
- ❑ Used his role as _____ effectively to influence decisions

❸ Met Standards (MS)

- ❑ Motivated and directed subordinates consistent with requirements
- ❑ Led discussions and administered discipline as required
- ❑ Exhibited a good level of self confidence in making decisions
- ❑ Was able to generate enthusiasm and an acceptable level of loyalty from subordinates
- ❑ Knew and followed organization regulations and values
- ❑ Was fair minded in assessing conflicts between subordinates
- ❑ Encouraged subordinates to participate in discussions and give their input
- ❑ Was effective in training subordinates to take leadership roles

- ❑ Could be counted on to put safety and proper procedures before production goals
- ❑ Overcame challenges to his authority while maintaining subordinates' respect

❷ Below Standards (BS)

- ❑ Was too slow in decision-making process, leaving coworkers and subordinates feeling insecure
- ❑ Needed to substantially increase his communications with coworkers and subordinates
- ❑ Did not step in to resolve conflicts until things had reached a boiling point
- ❑ Needed to be more proactive in getting input from coworkers and subordinates
- ❑ Exhibited hesitancy in taking a leadership role
- ❑ Did not try to elevate his profile throughout the organization
- ❑ Needed to get a better grasp on organizational policies, procedures, and values and communicate these to subordinates
- ❑ Struggled with setting goals and objectives
- ❑ Did not know when to exercise his role as leader

❶ Far Below Standards (FBS)

- ❑ Displayed an abrasive style of commanding subordinates
- ❑ Did not have the respect and loyalty of subordinates
- ❑ Had _____ subordinate complaints for failure to discipline fairly
- ❑ Failed to resolve subordinate conflicts
- ❑ Had no program to train subordinates
- ❑ Was unable to build strong teams
- ❑ Failed to get input from coworkers and subordinates
- ❑ Did not follow organizational policies
- ❑ Did not communicate and promote organizational values
- ❑ Used power and influence inappropriately
- ❑ Set unreasonably high standards for subordinates

❶ Not Observed (NO), Not Ratable (NR), Not Applicable (NA), Failed (F)

❏ Not observed

❏ Demonstrated unsuitability for a leadership role during this time

❏ Lacked the skills to function in this role

❏ Needed to be transferred to another position

❏ Failed to meet the minimum aptitude and requirements for this position

Recommended Action Steps for the Manager

- Review and adapt those goal steps at the end of this section that apply to increase this skill (see page 171) and present them to the employee.

- Present leadership training options to the employee for consideration.

- Ask the employee to write her career objectives and short- and long-term career goals involving the use of leadership skills.

- Have the employee outline in a plan for the next quarter exactly how he will pursue increasing his leadership role, and how that will be in evidence in concrete terms; and then have him sign it.

Learning Skills

Measuring how well an employee is learning the facts and skills of his job—particularly a new hire or transferred employee—is vital. Where the ability to constantly learn new material and skills is important, this should be weighted very high in assessing the employee's success in his performance in the position.

❺ Outstanding (O)

❏ Absorbed new information at an amazing rate

❏ Was eager to be challenged with new learning tasks

- ❑ Showed both outstanding progress in learning new material and also in applying it
- ❑ Was able to change gears easily and seamlessly to maximize learning and application skills
- ❑ Promoted embracing new learning among subordinates
- ❑ Was able to quickly teach what he learned
- ❑ Endorsed the continuing education program among subordinates

④ Exceeded Standards (ES)

- ❑ Learned new material and skills quickly and completely
- ❑ Displayed the ability to implement newly acquired information within a short time
- ❑ Promoted a learning environment among subordinates
- ❑ Was able to teach what he learned
- ❑ Could assimilate and fit new learning into present procedures
- ❑ Was committed to the continuing education program

③ Met Standards (MS)

- ❑ Established a training program for subordinates
- ❑ Offered subordinates opportunities for continuing education programs
- ❑ Had a record of implementing new procedures successfully ____% of the time
- ❑ Tested ____% in staff proficiency on new procedures
- ❑ Had a ____% satisfaction rating from subordinates for continuing education programs
- ❑ Was rated ____ out of a possible ____ in teaching skills by subordinates

② Below Standards (BS)

- ❑ Needed help in organizing and implementing continuing education programs
- ❑ Offered subordinates continuing education programs only ____ times, compared with ____ times in the last reporting period

- ❑ Implemented only ____ out of ____ new procedures
- ❑ Was rated "poor" in teaching skills by subordinates
- ❑ Tested ____% in staff proficiency on new procedures

❶ Far Below Standards (FBS)

- ❑ Did not learn from mistakes of the last reporting period
- ❑ Failed to implement a single continuing education program of the ____ required
- ❑ Did not promote or encourage subordinates to participate in learning opportunities
- ❑ Did not fulfill teaching function
- ❑ Received ratings of "very poor" in teaching skills from subordinates

⓪ Not Observed (NO), Not Ratable (NR), Not Applicable (NA), Failed (F)

- ❑ Not ratable
- ❑ Not applicable
- ❑ Failed to meet the minimum requirement

Recommended Action Steps for the Manager

- Review the steps at the end of this section (see page 171) and adapt those that can help the employee improve in this skill area.

- Have the employee write a personal plan to explain how he will make his learning skills requirements current and how he will meet these requirements of his position within the next quarter; then have him sign it.

Listening Skills

Every good communicator has excellent listening skills. It's important in every position where an employee must interact with others. Weight this skill commensurate with the listening skills needed by the employee to do his job well.

❺ Outstanding (O)

- ❑ Listened actively in a very focused way, summarized, and mirrored back to the speaker a brief summary of the salient points
- ❑ Asked excellent questions that aided understanding at the appropriate times during the listening process
- ❑ Organized the listening process for subordinates into productive segments, allowing for rebuttals and questions to advance dialogue and understanding
- ❑ Heard the speaker completely and did not interrupt
- ❑ Maintained eye contact and gave the speaker encouragement and reassurances that she was being heard
- ❑ Made a concerted effort to understand all other points of view
- ❑ Ensured that all group sessions were conducted so each contributor was given respect
- ❑ Invited all opinions and points of view while still controlling the session
- ❑ Had the ability to read the audience and ask questions others were too timid to voice
- ❑ Heard once and understood new information
- ❑ Recalled content of what was said with outstanding accuracy
- ❑ Was able to interpret and apply new information immediately
- ❑ Followed instructions and directions perfectly
- ❑ Demonstrated that he was genuinely interested in what others had to say

❹ Exceeded Standards (ES)

- ❑ Displayed good listening skills most of the time
- ❑ Demonstrated the ability to understand and summarize what the speaker said
- ❑ Did not interrupt or let her attention wander
- ❑ Showed a good grasp of new information presented and was able to put it into practice quickly
- ❑ Asked appropriate questions ____% of the time
- ❑ Recalled content of what was presented ____% of the time

- ❏ Demonstrated an active interest in others' opinions and points of view
- ❏ Helped subordinates develop the ability to hear and understand presentations by structuring sessions with time for questions

❸ Met Standards (MS)

- ❏ Was able to understand and follow presented instructions ____% of the time
- ❏ Could adequately summarize what had been verbally presented
- ❏ Did not usually interrupt during presentations
- ❏ Recalled ____% of the content given most of the time
- ❏ Asked questions when he didn't understand
- ❏ Showed respect for the opinions and views of others

❷ Below Standards (BS)

- ❏ Asked questions that were answered in the presentation
- ❏ Interrupted when others were speaking
- ❏ Failed to show interest in the opinions and views of others
- ❏ Was often dismissive of the opinions and views of others with whom he disagreed
- ❏ Needed to be the center of attention
- ❏ Became defensive when someone presented another point of view

❶ Far Below Standards (FBS)

- ❏ Did not absorb verbally presented material ____% of the time
- ❏ Needed visual aids and several verbal reviews in order to absorb information
- ❏ Was intolerant of others' opinions and points of view
- ❏ Interrupted repeatedly and disrupted verbal presentations
- ❏ Did not ask questions at appropriate times, or at all
- ❏ Misinterpreted what had been presented and was unable to summarize after a verbal presentation
- ❏ Demonstrated a very short attention span

❶ Not Observed (NO), Not Ratable (NR), Not Applicable (NA), Failed (F)

❏ Not observed

❏ Not ratable

❏ Failed

❏ Must be trained in listening skills in order to qualify for this position

Recommended Action Steps for the Manager

- Review the recommendations at the end of this section (see page 171) and adapt those that apply.

- Inform the employee of his need to improve his listening skills in order to maintain his job and/or be promoted.

- Have the employee record ____ verbal sessions, outline the presentations and write a summary for each.

- Require that the employee take notes during verbal presentations and practice with her when and how to ask appropriate questions.

- Have the employee write up a plan describing how he will improve his listening skills within the next quarter; then have him sign it, and schedule regular follow-up sessions to check on his progress.

Loyalty and Dedication

Loyalty and dedication are always important, but sometimes these attributes may be the most valuable soft skills an employee possesses. When assessing an employee's performance, these soft skills can compensate for weaker hard skills. For organizations that deliver services to their clients or patients, or for organizations that have proprietary information and/or products, these attributes play a much larger role in the employee review process than they do for a manufacturing organization, for example. Weight these attributes according to their importance to the employee's performance within your organization.

❺ Outstanding (O)

- ❑ Could always be counted on to put her job and the organization first
- ❑ Was completely committed to organizational goals and objectives
- ❑ Could be counted on to build loyalty among subordinates
- ❑ Instituted programs to recognize dedication and loyalty among subordinates
- ❑ Took great pride in the department and its employees
- ❑ Worked very hard to compensate for superiors' weaknesses

❹ Exceeded Standards (ES)

- ❑ Took pride in producing quality products
- ❑ Could be depended upon to stand up for subordinates
- ❑ Used subordinate recognition program to help build loyalty and dedication
- ❑ Would cover for the shortcomings of superiors to maintain a united front
- ❑ Put the welfare of the organization above personal goals
- ❑ Defended the organization's policies and objectives to subordinates, even if he disagreed
- ❑ Promoted team spirit within the department

❸ Met Standards (MS)

- ❑ Carried out the organization's policies and objectives
- ❑ Could be counted on to follow directives given by superiors
- ❑ Filled in intermittently for superiors who didn't meet their requirements
- ❑ Used the established program of recognition with subordinates occasionally
- ❑ Defended the work of subordinates from criticism by other departments
- ❑ Exhibited an acceptable level of producing quality products within the guidelines

❷ Below Standards (BS)

- ❏ Needed occasionally to be reminded to follow organization policies and objectives
- ❏ Challenged the directives of superiors on occasion
- ❏ Could not be counted on to always put the good of the organization above his personal goals
- ❏ Was unwilling to fill in for superiors when and where needed to make up for a shortfall
- ❏ Did not recognize acts of dedication and loyalty by subordinates as important to building his team
- ❏ Needed to work on promoting team spirit among subordinates

❶ Far Below Standards (FBS)

- ❏ Did not use the system of subordinate recognition to build loyalty and dedication
- ❏ Failed to recognize the need to follow organization policies and objectives
- ❏ Challenged superiors in front of subordinates on a regular basis
- ❏ Put personal goals ahead of the organization's goals
- ❏ Left gaps in coverage instead of filling in for superiors as directed
- ❏ Needed to put in place the program of recognizing subordinates

❶ Not Observed (NO), Not Ratable (NR), Not Applicable (NA), Failed (F)

- ❏ Not observed
- ❏ Failed to meet all minimum requirements in this regard
- ❏ Displayed an unacceptable attitude of disloyalty and lack of dedication

- Review the recommendations at the end of this section (see page 171) and adapt those that apply.

- Discuss with the employee the value placed on loyalty and dedication within the organization, and outline his shortcomings.

- Define specific areas where the employee can increase his loyalty and dedication.

- Ask the employee to write her own plan for how she will increase her sense of loyalty and dedication to the organization in the next quarter and list concrete objectives that will demonstrate her progress; have the employee sign her plan of action and arrange meetings to check periodically on progress.

Management Skills and Style

The ability to get the very best from subordinates, to maintain a positive work environment, and to act strategically in a timely and efficient manner are just some of the qualities of an employee with demonstrated management skills and style. Weight these qualities to reflect the management role the employee has in his job description.

5 Outstanding (O)

- ❑ Grasped the importance of his role in meeting the organization's overall goals and objectives

- ❑ Translated organizational goals and objectives into an excellent managerial program for his department

- ❑ Did outstanding short- and long-term planning

- ❑ Exercised excellent control over ordering supplies and materials to keep his subordinates producing at a high level

- ❑ Set objectives for subordinates and made sure they were met

- ❑ Inspired subordinates to a very high standard of achievement

- ❑ Maintained a positive work environment for his subordinates

- ❑ Was accepting and confident
- ❑ Provided subordinates and coworkers with constructive criticism
- ❑ Made fair and equitable work assignments
- ❑ Rewarded team performance
- ❑ Had a reputation for going far beyond the management requirements of his position
- ❑ Used all the direct and indirect channels for getting work accomplished
- ❑ Communicated the organization's goals and objectives in terms of achievable goals for his subordinates
- ❑ Was approachable and encouraged subordinates to contribute
- ❑ Recognized accomplishments of his subordinates in ways that inspired others
- ❑ Was known for fair and equitable dealings with all his subordinates

❹ Exceeded Standards (ES)
- ❑ Could be counted on to maintain calm in a crisis
- ❑ Set a high standard of achievement for himself and his subordinates
- ❑ Used recognition and rewards effectively to inspire subordinates ____% of the time
- ❑ Planned and organized well to keep production of subordinates consistently at ____%
- ❑ Showed no favoritism in dealing with and assigning work to subordinates
- ❑ Treated all employees equally and valued each employee's input
- ❑ Did a good job of reviewing subordinates' progress and career path plans
- ❑ Was willing to step in during times when the department was shorthanded to be sure the job got done
- ❑ Promoted enthusiasm for the job among subordinates
- ❑ Used every avenue available to keep his subordinates' work on track
- ❑ Encouraged subordinates to develop and grow their skill levels

- Provided constructive feedback most of the time
- Made good use of organizational resources to keep the department running smoothly

❸ Met Standards (MS)

- Held an acceptable record of ____% success in dealing with crises
- Had no complaints from subordinates of favoritism, discrimination, or other such issues
- Worked well with coworkers to resolve interdepartmental problems
- Kept production on schedule by planning and ordering supplies on time
- Maintained a positive work atmosphere for subordinates
- Kept an open-door policy to get subordinates' input and hear complaints
- Was fair in evaluating subordinates' work and progress
- Offered subordinates encouragement to develop and grow their job skills
- Would step in occasionally to make sure deadlines and output goals were met
- Had a good working knowledge of organization policies and procedures and used them with ____% success

❷ Below Standards (BS)

- Dealt with crises satisfactorily only ____% of the time
- Had ____ complaints of favoritism from subordinates
- Had ____ reports of conflicts with coworkers over interdepartmental issues
- Held a record of ____% below-production goals for the review period
- Did not deal with subordinate complaints ___% of the time (as reported by HR)
- Showed reluctance to complete subordinate reviews on time ____% of the time

- ❏ Failed to meet deadlines ____ times because of staff shortages that weren't covered
- ❏ Needed assistance from other departments in order to complete proper procedural requirements
- ❏ Had a departmental record of subordinate low morale
- ❏ Did not institute the organizational program of recognition for subordinates

❶ Far Below Standards (FBS)

- ❏ Had ____ complaints of favoritism and discrimination from subordinates
- ❏ Failed to set goals and monitor subordinates' progress ____% of the time
- ❏ Managed by using the fear principle
- ❏ Displayed an aloof and detached style that did not invite subordinates' input
- ❏ Did not possess leadership qualities that subordinates wanted to emulate
- ❏ Was inflexible and rigid in his approach and was unable to alter methods to meet crises
- ❏ Failed to meet production goals ____ times
- ❏ Was argumentative and abrupt with coworkers
- ❏ Did not entertain others' points of view
- ❏ Received ____ complaints for initiating conflicts with other departments
- ❏ Did not understand and employ organizational procedures
- ❏ Was delinquent in doing subordinates' performance reviews
- ❏ Had a turnover rate of ____% for subordinates
- ❏ Did not use the organization's recognition program for subordinates
- ❏ Made work assignments without giving subordinates proper training, supplies, or information ____% of the time
- ❏ Gave subordinates instructions by email rather than face-to-face

□ Was abrasive and confrontational in his approach _____% of the time

□ Did not participate in the production process of his department

❶ Not Observed (NO), Not Ratable (NR), Not Applicable (NA), Failed (F)

□ Not observed

□ Not applicable

□ Failed in his managerial role

Recommended Action Steps for the Manager

- Review the recommendations at the end of this section (see page 171) and adapt any that apply.

- Have the employee write up a plan that specifically states his management goals for the next quarter and how he will work to meet them; schedule a meeting to review his plan, make any necessary adjustments, and have the employee sign the final plan.

Motivation

The desire and drive to excel and achieve comes from a mix of internal and external factors—conscious and unconscious. The motivated employee is a great asset in any job. Weight this quality according to the part it plays in his job performance.

❺ Outstanding (O)

□ Influenced everyone around her positively with her desire to do exceptional work

□ Was eager to do outstanding work on every task and challenged himself to do each task to the highest standard

□ Needed only to get the assignment and was ready to tackle it

□ Displayed a very strong incentive to succeed

□ Infected all those around him with enthusiasm to perform at the highest level

- ❏ Kept flagging enthusiasm of others from affecting subordinates by inventing new incentives for them to aspire to
- ❏ Brought clear purpose and direction to each task
- ❏ Never doubted that she would achieve each goal set before her
- ❏ Had the strongest internal drive of any employee
- ❏ Was rated "high" on driving force by his coworkers and subordinates

❹ Exceeded Standards (ES)

- ❏ Translated assignments into challenges for his subordinates
- ❏ Raised the enthusiasm factor for even routine assignments
- ❏ Emphasized the need to do a good job regardless of the task
- ❏ Was rated "good" on getting subordinates to tackle undesirable jobs with purpose and resolve
- ❏ Helped subordinates focus on achieving a high standard in each task
- ❏ Brought a positive attitude and high energy to even routine tasks
- ❏ Excelled in bringing positive and productive zeal to each task
- ❏ Was very goal driven
- ❏ Did not wilt midway through long projects but kept the effort going until the goal was reached

❸ Met Standards (MS)

- ❏ Brought a good effort to each new assignment
- ❏ Added positive energy to the work atmosphere
- ❏ Could usually be counted on to deliver on a task even if faced with delays and obstacles
- ❏ Was able to muster internal energy for nearly every task though sometimes late in the process
- ❏ Did not quit on a project he had been assigned but did sometimes stagnate
- ❏ Faced challenges with internal resolve
- ❏ Could be focused on the goal if nudged by her supervisors

- ❏ Maintained task momentum under normal circumstances
- ❏ Stayed on task during stressful situations most of the time

❷ Below Standards (BS)

- ❏ Let his enthusiasm flag when faced with obstacles
- ❏ Turned negative when others failed to cooperate ____% of the time
- ❏ Got pulled off task in the face of obstacles and distractions
- ❏ Needed help in maintaining goal focus on the original task ____% of the time
- ❏ Was reluctant to take on additional assignments
- ❏ Did not respond to "pep talks" aimed at raising the enthusiasm level for a task
- ❏ Lacked the internal drive to set his own goals
- ❏ Did not seem to see beyond obstacles ____% of the time
- ❏ Depended on supervisor to give him a push to get all the way to the goal
- ❏ Supplied negative energy to team efforts ____% of the time

❶ Far Below Standards (FBS)

- ❏ Could not stay focused on the goal without continual prodding
- ❏ Stalled in his efforts to complete even routine tasks without continual prodding
- ❏ Brought negative energy to every team she was assigned to
- ❏ Did not have the necessary internal drive to push through his own apathy to get the task done; lacked the ability to work independently
- ❏ Refused to set goals for himself
- ❏ Failed to stay focused on even short-term projects
- ❏ Was not able to sustain enthusiasm to complete her work

❶ Not Observed (NO), Not Ratable (NR), Not Applicable (NA), Failed (F)

- ❏ Could not function in this position
- ❏ Not observed
- ❏ Failed to demonstrate motivation

Recommended Action Steps for the Manager

- Review with the employee his record for demonstrating motivation on the job during the review period. Use actual examples from your observations (recorded in your employee journal) and actual numbers you have gleaned from other records.

- Ask the employee for his explanation and response, but control the discussion to make sure it remains on track and productive.

- Assimilate the employee's input and then tell him what he needs to do to improve his motivation. Ask him what external factors in the workplace would help him be more motivated. Get to specifics in both areas.

- Here are suggestions you may want the employee to consider:
  - Make sure you understand each assignment and the goal before starting.
  - Listen completely to assignments and repeat them in your own words to your supervisor.
  - Challenge yourself to set your own internal goal for completing the task before deadline.
  - Create your own personal reward system to energize you to do the job well.
  - Be determined to be a positive team member and energizer on each task.

- Present possible sources available to the employee for learning this skill—either within the organization or through community or college training classes.

- Ask the employee to write up his personal plan for improving his motivation, including what external factors he feels would help motivate him; have him sign it, and schedule follow-up meetings for each week to review his progress.

Personal Style

The characteristics that make a person uniquely himself are a vital part of what makes each employee effective in his job—or not. Weight personal-style skills according to the impact they have on the employee's effectiveness in his job.

❺ Outstanding (O)

- ❑ Could always be counted on to act to the highest ethical standard
- ❑ Was able to remain objective and calm in all stressful situations
- ❑ Did an exceptional job of multitasking and keeping current on many details
- ❑ Used honesty and respect for others as his guiding principles
- ❑ Accepted constructive and destructive criticism graciously
- ❑ Was able to turn a very negative situation completely around through her ability to be tactful and understand the motive of the other person
- ❑ Had a keen ability to make the right decisions without delay
- ❑ Stood up for subordinates even when they made mistakes
- ❑ Admitted errors without excusing or blaming others and corrected those errors quickly
- ❑ Maintained a great sense of humor, even in difficult and stressful situations
- ❑ Drew others to himself
- ❑ Was willing to take on responsibility, even when the task had personal risk
- ❑ Made her personal code of moral behavior known without being abrasive or preachy
- ❑ Set an excellent standard of conduct for himself and example for his subordinates
- ❑ Insisted on acceptance of everyone in his department
- ❑ Found a way to do her work within the spirit and the letter of the organizational policies and procedures

- Exuded enthusiasm and a positive attitude that increased job satisfaction for subordinates
- Recognized the contributions of coworkers and subordinates in ways that honored them
- Was always looking for ways to do the job better, and always found them
- Put the organization goals and objectives first
- Possessed excellent team-building skills
- Made coworkers and subordinates feel at ease and able to brainstorm
- Welcomed input from everyone
- Was accepting and welcoming of all people and points of view
- Managed discussions and meetings expertly to keep them on target, on time, and productive
- Ran an orderly, neat, and safe work area
- Was extremely disciplined in his approach to any task
- Went the second mile to create positive working relationships with coworkers
- Received the highest marks from clients after presentations
- Resolved disagreements between subordinates and coworkers at a ____% success rate

❹ Exceeded Standards (ES)

- Set a high standard of ethics and honesty for subordinates
- Rewarded subordinates for contributions in meetings and discussions
- Was accepting of everyone and treated everyone equally
- Placed organizational goals, policies, and procedures first in getting the job done ____% of the time
- Used a good approach to team building among subordinates
- Took responsibility for her work
- Operated an organized and orderly work environment
- Received "good" reviews from coworkers and subordinates

- ❏ Set aside time during the workday to receive input from subordinates and discuss conflicts
- ❏ Used the program of subordinate recognition effectively
- ❏ Could handle two or three ongoing projects effectively
- ❏ Created a positive work environment for subordinates most of the time
- ❏ Was rated "good" by clients for his presentations
- ❏ Tracked well in following up on details
- ❏ Was disciplined in his approach to getting the job done
- ❏ Acted in a timely manner to resolve disputes, conflicts, and disagreements among subordinates
- ❏ Did not shirk his responsibilities
- ❏ Looked for ways to do her job better
- ❏ Worked with a high level of energy and determination
- ❏ Displayed humor in situations of stress and conflict, which served to improve productivity

❸ Met Standards (MS)

- ❏ Made decisions consistent with organizational procedures and policies
- ❏ Worked harmoniously with other departments and coworkers
- ❏ Owned a reputation for personal integrity
- ❏ Expressed enthusiasm for his job
- ❏ Could multitask at an acceptable level
- ❏ Instituted _____ new techniques to streamline production
- ❏ Used organizational recognition program for subordinates
- ❏ Had a minimum of conflicts with coworkers and subordinates
- ❏ Made _____ changes in procedures to make them comply with organizational policies
- ❏ Received _____ complaints by subordinates, which she resolved satisfactorily
- ❏ Tried to elicit input from subordinates during meetings and discussions _____% of the time

- ❑ Did not show favoritism or discriminate
- ❑ Set a high standard for honesty and ethical behavior within the department
- ❑ Negotiated with other departments for distribution of work
- ❑ Acted responsibly in setting deadlines and goals

❷ Below Standards (BS)

- ❑ Was very defensive in the face of constructive criticism
- ❑ Lacked enthusiasm for his work
- ❑ Needed outside help in identifying trouble spots and seeking ways to improve production
- ❑ Had ____ subordinate complaints for lack of diversity and favoritism
- ❑ Failed to involve subordinates in the process of giving input during meetings and discussions
- ❑ Showed a personal style of inflexibility and a need for control
- ❑ Used sarcasm and off-color humor in the workplace
- ❑ Received ____ coworker complaints for being difficult to work with, withdrawn, moody, and cynical
- ❑ Got bogged down in unnecessary details
- ❑ Wasted a lot of time and production potential by not planning and ordering supplies in a timely manner
- ❑ Worked amid clutter and chaos, which negatively impacted production and quality control
- ❑ Was known to spread gossip and rumors
- ❑ Let serious infractions by subordinates slip, then came down hard on something insignificant
- ❑ Was unable to prioritize ____% of the time
- ❑ Did not have the necessary respect of her team
- ❑ Was not able to step in to help subordinates meet deadlines
- ❑ Failed to resolve conflicts between subordinates ____ times

❶ Far Below Standards (FBS)

- ❏ Did not meet the essential minimal standard for ethical behavior
- ❏ Had _____ violations for not following organizational policies and procedures during the review period
- ❏ Was unpredictable in his behavior, leaving subordinates feeling like they were walking on eggshells
- ❏ Used only an authoritarian personal style
- ❏ Was intolerant of most points of view that didn't align with hers
- ❏ Isolated himself and didn't communicate with coworkers or subordinates
- ❏ Was often argumentative and abrasive with coworkers
- ❏ Had _____ complaints registered by subordinates for showing favoritism and discrimination in the review period
- ❏ Used threats and coercion to get subordinates to increase production
- ❏ Engaged in gossip and rumors to build alliances with subordinates
- ❏ Let infractions go undisciplined, then came down hard
- ❏ Was too focused on minute details and couldn't see the big picture
- ❏ Was not able to perform the planning functions needed
- ❏ Failed to maintain a safe and orderly work area
- ❏ Couldn't accept constructive criticism
- ❏ Created a negative work environment
- ❏ Ignored disputes between subordinates and refused to mediate

❶ Not Observed (NO), Not Ratable (NR), Not Applicable (NA), Failed (F)

- ❏ Not observed
- ❏ Not ratable
- ❏ Not applicable
- ❏ Failed to perform in this role

- Review the recommendation steps at the end of this section (see page 171) and adapt any that will help the employee improve.

- Ask the employee to write up his personal plan for overcoming deficits and developing an effective personal style to be achieved in the next quarter, and set up a schedule of meetings to check on his progress.

Planning, Organizing, and Scheduling

The exercise that charts a path from the present status to a projected future goal is usually divided into short-term and long-term increments. Translating that plan into action steps to be taken requires that allocations for supplies and personnel be made. In measuring his performance level, weight how much of the employee's job description depends upon this ability.

❺ Outstanding (O)

❑ Excelled in both short- and long-term planning

❑ Developed comprehensive and attainable short- and long-term plans

❑ Gave proper consideration to all contingencies in developing plans

❑ Was very skilled in translating goals into sound strategies and the actionable steps to achieve them

❑ Built allowances for delays and problems into his plans

❑ Kept work on schedule by masterful organization and staffing

❑ Was very adept at rescheduling to accommodate unexpected changes and delays

❑ Coordinated expertly with other departments to meet scheduling requirements

④ Exceeded Standards (ES)

- ❑ Coordinated schedules with other departments to avoid conflicts
- ❑ Had a good handle on output and didn't overcommit
- ❑ Made contingency plans that worked seamlessly
- ❑ Kept focused on the long-term plan in day-to-day scheduling and production planning
- ❑ Used scheduling and staffing tools proficiently

③ Met Standards (MS)

- ❑ Created long- and short-term plans with acceptable proficiency
- ❑ Was accurate ____% of the time in his staffing predictions
- ❑ Used scheduling and staffing tools with an acceptable proficiency rate
- ❑ Had a good record of ____% success in implementing contingency plans as needed
- ❑ Coordinated schedules with other departments to avoid conflicts at a success rate of ____%

② Below Standards (BS)

- ❑ Got bogged down in minute details and couldn't transition to long- or even short-term planning
- ❑ Created staffing and supply crises for other departments due to poor scheduling ____ times
- ❑ Did not learn how to use the scheduling and staffing tools properly
- ❑ Had no contingency plan ____% of the time
- ❑ Did not plan effectively to meet peak demands
- ❑ Operated in a state of chaos due to lack of planning

① Far Below Standards (FBS)

- ❑ Committed staffing errors that cost the organization _____
- ❑ Did not know how to use the scheduling, staffing, and projection tools
- ❑ Created a crisis due to not planning properly for delivery of supplies

- ❏ Failed to create a workable contingency plan
- ❏ Did not have the skills to perform the requirements of his job description

⓿ Not Observed (NO), Not Ratable (NR), Not Applicable (NA), Failed (F)

- ❏ Not observed
- ❏ Was not capable of performing this skill
- ❏ Not ratable
- ❏ Failed

Recommended Action Steps for the Manager

- ▪ Review the recommendations at the end of this section (see page 171) and adapt those that apply.
- ▪ Ask the employee to write up a plan for how he will work to improve his planning, organizing, and scheduling skills in the next quarter, including what his target goals for achievement will be, and have him sign it; schedule periodic meetings to check his progress.

Problem Solving

Working through the elements or details of a problem to reach a solution may include any number of hard skills, but it will most certainly also be a gauge of the employee's critical thinking skills.

❺ Outstanding (O)

- ❏ Understood that problems are a part of the process, anticipated areas where problems might occur with ____% accuracy, and constructed alternate plans to deal with them, should they occur
- ❏ Developed approaches that eliminated or minimized potential problems
- ❏ Explained clearly and completely to customers all the potential problem areas, and then offered possible solutions

- Was able to consistently develop practical and efficient solutions
- Recommended several possible solutions to a problem ____% of the time
- Took on problems others avoided and efficiently solved them
- Kept coworkers appraised of the status of problems, corrective actions, and possible outcomes
- Used a "no surprises" approach in keeping clients informed about the status of problems and solutions in a way that gave them confidence that she had things under control
- Broke down each problem into its component parts and solved it
- Built solutions into his project budget
- Did not let problems become an excuse for not producing on time
- Took on problems in a timely manner to avoid additional costs

❹ Exceeded Standards (ES)

- Employed diverse approaches to solve problems ____% of the time
- Was ____% effective in anticipating possible problems and planning for them
- Kept customers informed of possible problems, solutions, and outcomes
- Used sound analytical thinking to solve problems
- Broke problems down into their component parts and solved them ____% of the time
- Did not delay or hesitate in identifying a problem and moving to solve it
- Isolated problem elements, made effective changes, and often got a project back on track
- Alerted all the necessary departments affected when a problem occurred
- Made sure corrective steps were incorporated into future procedures where applicable
- Weighed the cost/benefit factors of possible solutions carefully
- Kept problems in proper perspective
- Approached problems as challenges he was eager and able to solve

❸ Met Standards (MS)

- ❏ Employed sound logic in developing solutions to problems ____% of the time

- ❏ Looked for underlying causes for problems in order to avoid them in the future

- ❏ Made sure solutions initiated a change in procedure when applicable

- ❏ Informed clients about possible problems, solutions, cost factors, and time delays at a ____% accuracy rate

- ❏ Was able to anticipate possible problems with ____% accuracy

- ❏ Took steps to initiate solutions in a timely fashion ____% of the time

- ❏ Calculated the cost factors involved in implementing solutions with ____% accuracy

- ❏ Was not afraid to take on a problem others had created ____% of the time

- ❏ Kept coworkers informed of the status of solutions on a need-to-know basis

❷ Below Standards (BS)

- ❏ Hesitated to take action when a problem was developing ____% of the time

- ❏ Came up with ineffective solutions ____% of the time

- ❏ Did not see the underlying procedural or systemic issues that were creating problems

- ❏ Stopped short of doing a complete analysis to ensure problems wouldn't recur ____% of the time

- ❏ Failed to make appropriate changes to procedures after problems had been solved

- ❏ Got fixated on one step in the solution process and lost sight of the whole process

- ❏ Did not keep the client informed about possible problems, solutions, and the possible effects on outcome, costs, and the time line

- ❏ Failed to get needed input from coworkers in order to create the best solution

❶ Far Below Standards (FBS)

- ❏ Was unable to anticipate possible problems adequately
- ❏ Delayed the initiation of the steps of a solution even when he had one
- ❏ Did not seek the input of coworkers when a problem occurred, and ignored it until it became a crisis ____% of the time
- ❏ Failed to inform the client when a project went off the rails until after a tenable solution could be reached
- ❏ Did not correctly analyze the problem ____% of the time
- ❏ Was not proactive in keeping coworkers informed when a problem occurred
- ❏ Did not see the wider procedural or systemic implication of a problem ____% of the time

❶ Not Observed (NO), Not Ratable (NR), Not Applicable (NA), Failed (F)

- ❏ Failed to take action and let problems spiral out of control
- ❏ Not observed
- ❏ Not applicable

Recommended Action Steps for the Manager

- ■ Review the recommendations at the end of this section (see page 171), and adapt those that apply.
- ■ Review in detail the problems and the solutions the employee has worked on over the review period.
- ■ Ask the employee to write a personal plan describing how he will continue to develop problem-solving skills, in specific terms, over the next quarter, and then have him sign the plan.

Productivity

Whatever the employee's job description, she needs to contribute in a way that helps the organization meet its expectations, coworkers and related departments meet their objectives, and helps her continue to develop her productivity skills. Weighting the employee's output must be done in relation to these considerations.

❺ Outstanding (O)

- ❏ Exceeded productivity targets consistently
- ❏ Maintained peak performance
- ❏ Produced high-quality products
- ❏ Set new production records regularly
- ❏ Surpassed expectations for volume and quality
- ❏ Motivated coworkers to higher quality and production
- ❏ Did not sacrifice quality to increase production
- ❏ Received the highest marks from customers for quality results
- ❏ Outperformed his coworkers on a consistent basis
- ❏ Hit the right balance between quality and productivity
- ❏ Was eager to take on new work that demanded a high degree of learning

❹ Exceeded Standards (ES)

- ❏ Took pride in leading in productivity
- ❏ Maintained a high output standard of between ____% and ____%, even when given a new task
- ❏ Was always eager to take on the challenge of remaining a top producer
- ❏ Coordinated her production with related departments
- ❏ Received high marks of ____% satisfaction from customers for quality results and response rate
- ❏ Kept the quality level at ____%, while meeting productivity goals
- ❏ Took on new work without complaint
- ❏ Helped motivate coworkers to increase their production by setting a good example

❸ Met Standards (MS)

- ❏ Produced as expected
- ❏ Met production goals on a regular basis
- ❏ Maintained production that met quality control standards
- ❏ Received acceptable marks of ____% satisfaction from customers for quality results and response rate
- ❏ Had a minimum of products returned because of quality issues
- ❏ Helped keep morale of coworkers up and production on target
- ❏ Worked well with coworkers and related departments to keep production on schedule

❷ Below Standards (BS)

- ❏ Had ____ reports of below-quota production by ____% to ____%
- ❏ Did not meet production goals on a regular basis
- ❏ Received ____ quality complaints from related departments during the review period
- ❏ Had a waste factor above acceptable range
- ❏ Lagged behind coworkers in production by ____%
- ❏ Continued with an error rate of ____%, even after additional training
- ❏ Arrived at work unfit to do his job
- ❏ Was unable to troubleshoot the higher-than-average error rate of his department

❶ Far Below Standards (FBS)

- ❏ Lost the ability to produce near his daily quota and was producing at ____% of acceptable standard
- ❏ Was not qualified to keep pace with the minimum production demands
- ❏ Produced at an unacceptable rate of ____% below the minimum
- ❏ Had a scrap rate of ____% above the acceptable level
- ❏ Displayed a disruptive attitude and influence on coworkers

- ❏ Impacted related departments in a negative way
- ❏ Failed to keep subordinates working due to poor production planning
- ❏ Was not able to troubleshoot the source of insufficient production
- ❏ Could not account for waste within his department
- ❏ Was unable to schedule the production rate of her subordinates

⓿ Not Observed (NO), Not Ratable (NR), Not Applicable (NA), Failed (F)

- ❏ Did not demonstrate that he could function in this role
- ❏ Not observed
- ❏ Not applicable
- ❏ Failed to meet the minimum standard

Recommended Action Steps for the Manager

- ■ Review employee's productivity in real terms and rate it with hard numbers whenever possible.
- ■ Allow the employee to give his input and response to explain his productivity numbers.
- ■ Cycle the employee through the in-service training program, or efficiency analysis, when that is appropriate.
- ■ Arrange a mentorship with another employee who excels in a parallel position, can inspire the employee, and can help the employee raise his levels and goals.
- ■ Present the employee with options he should consider in order to raise his production performance and advance his career path.
- ■ Have the employee write up his own personal production goals for the next quarter with hard numbers and outcomes, whenever possible; have him sign it; and schedule weekly meetings to review his progress.

Professionalism

The qualities of professional excellence and competence that are expected of the employee will depend upon his role. If the employee represents the organization to clients and customers, part of the professionalism measurement will include how she dresses, the grammar she uses, how she conducts herself, and whether or not her clients and customers get a positive impression of the organization from their interactions with her. If the employee works on an assembly line, a much higher grade will be given to the quality of the piece of production for which she is responsible and whether she gets along well with coworkers. To weight the professionalism of an employee, identify those key factors within the job description that mean doing it well.

❺ Outstanding (O)
- ❏ Demonstrated a confidence that was contagious when interacting with clients, making them want to do business with the organization
- ❏ Always set the standard high for dressing and grooming impeccably well and consistent with peer professional ideals
- ❏ Was always upbeat and positive in her interactions with clients
- ❏ Was a great ambassador for the organization when meeting with potential clients and customers
- ❏ Went far beyond the requirements in order to be sure clients were satisfied
- ❏ Created "friends" of the organization by his bright and sunny personality and exceptional standard of conduct
- ❏ Considered the assessments, criticism, and comments of coworkers very carefully and openly
- ❏ Did not discriminate or treat subordinates with favoritism
- ❏ Had a reputation for fair play with coworkers
- ❏ Knew the organization's products inside out, up and down

- ❏ Could be counted on to be open, honest, and direct in dealing with coworkers
- ❏ Made excellent presentations
- ❏ Knew the policies, procedures, and soul of the organization completely
- ❏ Was a standard bearer for professional behavior wherever he was
- ❏ Led by example in providing a role model for subordinates
- ❏ Maintained focus and calm under stressful situations
- ❏ Spoke to the level of his audience to get her message across
- ❏ Treated everyone with respect and dignity, regardless of their level or the situation
- ❏ Showed a generosity of spirit toward all those with whom he interrelated
- ❏ Took the organization position in every situation and was very persuasive in explaining it

❹ Exceeded Standards (ES)

- ❏ Dressed in a professional manner and was always well-groomed
- ❏ Comported himself with a friendly and open smile and greeting
- ❏ Had a reputation with clients for being a straight shooter but did it tactfully
- ❏ Knew product information and delivered it well
- ❏ Reviewed by peers and subordinates as highly professional in all her dealings with them
- ❏ Took the initiative to address situations when clients had questions or problems
- ❏ Behaved in a professional manner, regardless of the situation or environment—business or social
- ❏ Had a good handle on organization policies and procedures and their interpretation
- ❏ Represented the organization in a positive manner
- ❏ Could be counted on to be on time, ready for business, and prepared
- ❏ Received "above average" ratings from audiences after presentations

- ❑ Treated all levels of coworkers and subordinates with respect and dignity
- ❑ Was usually able to speak to the level of his audience

③ Met Standards (MS)

- ❑ Dressed within the guidelines for professional attire for his position and was usually well-groomed
- ❑ Received "average" reviews from clients for being able to answer questions and address problems
- ❑ Had a satisfactory grasp of product knowledge and presentation
- ❑ Received less than ____ complaints from coworkers or subordinates for unprofessional behavior
- ❑ Was on time to meetings and ready to participate ____% of the time
- ❑ Received a ____% satisfaction rating from customers for handling disputes
- ❑ Defended organization policies and procedures most of the time, even when it was difficult
- ❑ Accepted constructive criticism gracefully most of the time
- ❑ Treated coworkers and subordinates with respect and dignity
- ❑ Used audience-appropriate language in describing products and procedures
- ❑ Carried out promises for product delivery ___% of the time
- ❑ Was able to function satisfactorily in stressful situations

② Below Standards (BS)

- ❑ Had a record of below average (____%) for meeting guidelines for professional attire for his position
- ❑ Showed up for work improperly dressed and/or groomed ____% of the time
- ❑ Delivered on promised deadlines only ____% of the time
- ❑ Received ____ customer complaints for failing to solve problems or answer questions

- ❏ Arrived at meetings late and unprepared to participate ____% of the time

- ❏ Received complaints of deal-making outside organization policy on ____ occasions for the review period

- ❏ Did not adhere to organizational policy and procedure ____ times in the review period

- ❏ Used questionable ethics in dealings with coworkers and subordinates in order to better his own record

- ❏ Received ____ complaints for favoritism from subordinates

- ❏ Received ____ complaints for being abrasive and argumentative with coworkers and subordinates

- ❏ Held a grudge and refused to cooperate with coworkers ____% of the time

- ❏ Received ____ complaints for using unacceptable language with subordinates and coworkers

- ❏ Failed to answer customer requests and questions ____ times during the review period

❶ Far Below Standards (FBS)

- ❏ Showed up for work improperly dressed and/or groomed ____ times in the review period

- ❏ Did not meet the minimum hygiene standards for this position

- ❏ Did not create a professional appearance in his manner of dress, even after ____ warnings

- ❏ Displayed a complete disregard for organizational policies and procedures

- ❏ Failed to deliver on deadline ____ times during the review period

- ❏ Received ____ coworker and subordinate complaints for improper personal references and overfamiliarity

- ❏ Failed to follow organizational policy and procedures ____ times during the review period

- ❏ Received reports of "bad mouthing" the organization from customers ____ times

- ❑ Had disciplinary action pending for racial and sexist comments to subordinates
- ❑ Did not show up at meetings and/or was unprepared to participate ____% of the time
- ❑ Lost ____ customers due to unprofessional behavior
- ❑ Caused ____ subordinates to resign due to his failure to resolve disputes

🄾 Not Observed (NO), Not Ratable (NR), Not Applicable (NA), Failed (F)

- ❑ Failed to meet the minimum professional requirements for this position
- ❑ Not observed
- ❑ Not ratable
- ❑ Could not function in this position

Recommended Action Steps for the Manager

- ■ Review the recommendations at the end of this section (see page 171) and adapt those that apply.

Quality of Work

Whatever the job, producing outputs that meet the objectives of the organization, and continuing to produce them, involves a number of skills of measurement, detection, and correction. Weight this skill with real numbers/scores whenever possible.

🄾 Outstanding (O)

- ❑ Promoted the highest quality in everything he did
- ❑ Went the extra mile to ensure that customers were completely satisfied with the quality of the products they received
- ❑ Had zero tolerance for producing inferior products
- ❑ Documented all processes and procedures

- Reduced waste and scrap by ____%
- Put the highest priority on the organization's reputation for producing quality products
- Recognized the importance of quality in making sure the organization maintained its competitive edge
- Developed a bonus program for his subordinates that rewarded error-free production
- Was always vigilant to prevent any possible dip in quality
- Monitored everything from raw materials to finished products to avoid loss of quality and errors
- Practiced the principle that doing it right the first time can mean both top quality and profitability
- Used all the tools of quality control expertly to produce both quality and quantity
- Stayed late to make sure the job was done right
- Repeated quality production within a ____% margin
- Kept impeccable production and quality control records
- Maintained the highest quality and the highest morale among subordinates
- Took extreme personal pride in error-free work
- Received the highest rating for service from customers

❹ Exceeded Standards (ES)

- Remained committed to producing the best quality in difficult circumstances
- Knew how to improve the product to meet customer needs
- Relied on her high standard for achievement to ensure all the details were done to customer satisfaction
- Employed the organization's program to recognize high quality with subordinates
- Espoused to coworkers and subordinates the benefits of producing high quality the first time

- ❏ Emphasized preventing defects and inferior products
- ❏ Originated ＿＿＿ programs to reward his coworkers and subordinates who came up with quality-improvement recommendations
- ❏ Encouraged quality improvement throughout the organization
- ❏ Did not accept inferior raw materials or an error rate of over ＿＿＿%
- ❏ Set high standards for own work and that of subordinates

❸ Met Standards (MS)

- ❏ Had an error rate of between ＿＿＿% and ＿＿＿% reported by customers
- ❏ Received an overall satisfaction rating of ＿＿＿% from customers
- ❏ Used the measurement tools available to maintain an acceptable quality rating of ＿＿＿%
- ❏ Had a record of keeping cost factors at or below the acceptable level of ＿＿＿%
- ❏ Organized the work to maintain productivity
- ❏ Avoided downtime and remained focused on quality production
- ❏ Set a good example for subordinates about doing quality work
- ❏ Assisted coworkers and subordinates when necessary to maintain quality
- ❏ Kept accuracy and production between ＿＿＿% and ＿＿＿%
- ❏ Reduced errors and waste to ＿＿＿% as part of his operating policy
- ❏ Coordinated with coworkers to ensure that overall quality met acceptable standards
- ❏ Inspected, monitored, and tested raw materials regularly to ensure quality standards were maintained

❷ Below Standards (BS)

- ❏ Took too long to analyze problems when they occurred
- ❏ Had ＿＿＿ products returned by customers in the review period due to unacceptable quality

- Had scrap and waste figures of between ____% and ____% for the review period
- Turned out ____% reduced production when defects were factored in
- Required help from two other departments to meet production schedule
- Had cost overruns of ____% for the review period because of waste
- Let production fall by ____% in order to meet the minimum quality standard of ____%
- Turned in figures of a net loss due to return of products with defects or missing parts
- Alienated subordinates and coworkers by not adhering to the organization's acceptable quality standards
- Did not adequately monitor for quality output
- Did not institute the organization's quality-control program for subordinates

❶ Far Below Standards (FBS)
- Produced waste and scrap figures of between ____% and ____%, exceeding industry standards by ____% for the review period
- Ignored the organization's quality standards
- Alienated coworkers and subordinates by refusal to use quality-control tools of measurement or document procedure
- Produced an error rate of ____% for the review period
- Had ____ customer complaints of product defects for the review period
- Netted a loss of ____ for the review period because of high waste factors
- Did not use the organization's bonus program for increased quality with subordinates as directed
- Did not view quality as a priority
- Was not able to set and maintain quality standards

⓪ Not Observed (NO), Not Ratable (NR), Not Applicable (NA), Failed (F)

- ❏ Failed to meet the minimum quality standards of this position
- ❏ Not observed
- ❏ Not ratable
- ❏ Was not able to handle the requirements of this position

Recommended Action Steps for the Manager

- ■ Review the recommendations at the end of this section (see page 171) and adapt those that apply.
- ■ Review areas where quality is lacking with the employee and cite specific examples from his work in real numbers.

Recruiting

Identifying and hiring the best-qualified candidate, or enlisting coworkers or subordinates for a position or task—all in a timely and cost-effective manner—takes a special skill set. Weight it consistent with the position's demand for the skill.

❺ Outstanding (O)

- ❏ Demonstrated a superior ability to secure the perfect candidate for a position or function
- ❏ Used a great variety of innovative techniques, including advertising and making contacts, to attract the right candidates
- ❏ Knew how to motivate candidates to self-select for a position
- ❏ Had complete knowledge of all the legal requirements for all phases of the recruiting and hiring process
- ❏ Covered all the bases with applicants for a position or task
- ❏ Had only a ____% turnover rate for new hires and employees in new positions

- ❑ Received the highest marks from applicants for her recruiting methods and skills
- ❑ Conveyed to candidates a concise but in-depth review of position requirements, and organization benefits and policies
- ❑ Interviewed candidates in a comprehensive and analytical manner
- ❑ Made successful candidate selections in a minimum of time with ____% accuracy
- ❑ Knew exactly the right questions to ask
- ❑ Followed up with candidates at every step in the process
- ❑ Evaluated and hired candidates from within the organization with ____% success rate

❹ Exceeded Standards (ES)

- ❑ Was able to make several finalist selections from scores of applicants with ease
- ❑ Had a success rate of ____% to ____% in attracting the right candidates with his first ad or announcement
- ❑ Received "good" reviews for interview technique from ____% of candidates she interviewed
- ❑ Understood government requirements and regulations for the entire recruiting process and adhered to them
- ❑ Did a good job of placing ads and announcements in places that attracted good candidates
- ❑ Kept candidates informed about their status in the selection process
- ❑ Used good techniques to attract and evaluate candidates from within the organization
- ❑ Had a ____% success rate for hiring qualified applicants
- ❑ Received a score of ____% from applicants for covering all the aspects of the position
- ❑ Made a concerted effort to ask exemplary employees for referrals for new openings
- ❑ Did a good job of eliminating unqualified applicants

❸ Met Standards (MS)

- ❏ Met the requisite time frame for filling openings
- ❏ Complied with all legal regulations and requirements for every phase of the recruiting process
- ❏ Did an acceptable job of casting a wide net to get the right applicants
- ❏ Had a ____% success rate in hiring qualified applicants
- ❏ Experienced a ____% turnover rate among his new hires for the review period
- ❏ Used effectively in-service bulletin boards and online job websites to notify employees of new positions
- ❏ Received a ____% score from interviewees for his interview technique
- ❏ Did a good job of keeping finalists informed about the selection decision

❷ Below Standards (BS)

- ❏ Had to extend the selection process and hiring time frame ____ times during the review period
- ❏ Met the deadline for hiring only ____ times out of ____ for the review period
- ❏ Lost the best candidates for ____ positions due to mishandling the recruiting process
- ❏ Did not comply with all the legal regulations and requirements for every phase of the recruiting process
- ❏ Managed to get only a handful of applicants for ____ positions during the review period
- ❏ Received ____ follow-up calls with questions from interviewees after interviews
- ❏ Had a score of ____% of interviewees who stated his explanation of the position was incomplete, confusing, or lacked pertinent details
- ❏ Had a ____% turnover rate among her new hires for the review period

❶ Far Below Standards (FBS)

❑ Did not fill ____ positions during the review period

❑ Violated ____ government regulations and requirements during the recruiting process

❑ Failed to advertise the position in the proper places to get qualified candidates

❑ Did not inform employees about the openings in ____ cases and failed to ask employees for referrals

❑ Received scores of questions and complaints from applicants for his mishandling of the interview process, did not follow up as promised, and did not ask pertinent questions during the interviews

❑ Had a turnover rate among new hires of ____% during the review period

❶ Not Observed (NO), Not Ratable (NR), Not Applicable (NA), Failed (F)

❑ Not observed

❑ Not applicable

❑ Demonstrated that he is not equipped for this role

Recommended Action Steps for the Manager

- Review the recommendations at the end of this section (see page 171) and adapt those that apply.

- Review with the employee the areas where he can improve using hard numbers and real examples from his performance whenever possible; then ask the employee for his response.

Researching, Networking, and Resourcefulness

The employee who is fearless in facing any task with the full confidence that he will find a way to solve any problem, and then does so, is priceless. Weight this skill according to the requirement for it in the position.

⑤ Outstanding (O)

❑ Demonstrated an abundant amount of self-reliance in her ability to locate sources for anything

❑ Could find the best resource for anything, and quickly

❑ Was never stymied by a problem

❑ Developed a great network of peers at competitive and noncompetitive organizations

❑ Had an uncanny ability to evaluate sources and select only the best

❑ Anticipated when and where additional sources and resources might be needed and was ready with a supply

❑ Turned unlikely sources into a support team by coming up with win-win solutions

❑ Used a combination of unusual sources to develop innovative new solutions and cost-saving results

❑ Surpassed targets and delivered early on deadlines on a regular basis

❑ Had extraordinary online research skills that he used expertly to find needed information

❑ Widened and broadened the scope of organizational sources

❑ Raised the organization's profile and prestige in the industry through his resourcefulness and networking

④ Exceeded Standards (ES)

❑ Made full use of organizational resources and applied them in unique ways

❑ Allocated resources wisely

- Met deadlines easily and routinely
- Hit targets regularly
- Found ways of doing his job under pressure without drama or trauma
- Employed economies of scale to solve production problems
- Zeroed in on possible solutions quickly and effectively
- Unearthed solutions when others failed
- Evaluated information quickly and easily
- Demonstrated good online research skills

❸ Met Standards (MS)

- Was capable of finding resources to solve his problems ____% of the time
- Met deadlines on time
- Could find sources online at an acceptable rate
- Used organizational resources at an acceptable level
- Made good use of association connections
- Produced as targeted and on deadline ____% of the time
- Showed aptitude to increase his ability to be more resourceful

❷ Below Standards (BS)

- Performed slightly behind the curve in planning for upcoming needs
- Would not share sources and resources with coworkers
- Came in above budget by ____% to ____% more than ____ times out of ____
- Needed to substantially improve online research skills
- Depended on others to do the research and resourcing for him
- Requested additional resources ____% of the time
- Did not use organizational resources nearly enough
- Failed to properly use the research tools available ____% of the time
- Did not always grasp research information supplied to her
- Was slow to admit when he didn't understand

❑ Failed to ask pertinent questions in order to come up with the right resources

❑ Did not use allocated resources well

❑ Underutilized organization resources

❶ Far Below Standards (FBS)

❑ Was unable to evaluate resources and make the best selection

❑ Did not know how to do online research

❑ Depended on the buddy system for information instead of doing original research

❑ Failed to use organizational resources and contacts as required

❑ Operated over budget ____% of the time

❑ Did not meet deadlines or targets ____ times out of ____

❑ Refused to accept resource recommendations from coworkers

❑ Viewed his resources as proprietary and would not share them with coworkers

❑ Misinterpreted data ____ times out of ____ times

⓿ Not Observed (NO), Not Ratable (NR), Not Applicable (NA), Failed (F)

❑ Not observed

❑ Failed to meet the minimum standard for resourcefulness

❑ Did not demonstrate that he can function in this position

Recommended Action Steps for the Manager

- See suggestions at the end of this section (page 171), and include those that apply.

- Ask the employee to create a specific set of goals for how he will use to improve his research, networking, and resourcefulness skills; these lists should start with real names of people he will contact, as well as sources for research and a plan to become more resourceful.

- Meet with the employee and review and approve his lists; set dates for completion and follow-up; and arrange meetings to review and adjust those goals each week.

Safety

Awareness and procedures for keeping employees healthy and free from harm in the workplace are invaluable and should be weighted in the overall performance review based on the employee's need for this skill.

❺ Outstanding (O)

- ❏ Received the organization's top safety award for zero infractions
- ❏ Perceived potential safety hazards and instituted preventive measures
- ❏ Was active on industry-wide safety committees and panels and presented to them on a regular basis
- ❏ Promoted increased safety measures by showing cost benefits and increased production outcomes
- ❏ Reduced the accident rate per employee by ____% for the review period
- ❏ Monitored carefully all outside visitors to areas where safety gear is required
- ❏ Was proactive in reporting industry-wide safety issues to the proper government authorities
- ❏ Insisted that all his subordinates know CPR, know how to operate lifesaving equipment, and take and pass the safety-training course
- ❏ Followed organizational safety rules and security regulations and practiced them to the letter and added a few of his own for his department
- ❏ Took proactive steps to prevent safety hazards
- ❏ Insisted on top-of-the-mind attention by subordinates to safety first at all times
- ❏ Ran safety drills in his department on a regular basis
- ❏ Complied with all OSHA requirements and regulations
- ❏ Maintained a record of zero tolerance for safety infractions

- ❑ Created a taskforce within his department to be vigilant in looking for potential safety problems and to create safer ways to perform their jobs
- ❑ Required that safety gear be worn in the production area at all times
- ❑ Posted safety reminders in all subordinate work areas
- ❑ Instituted a safety recognition program for subordinates that operates all the time

❹ Exceeded Standards (ES)

- ❑ Was vigilant in following all OSHA requirements and regulations
- ❑ Made sure safety reminder posters were prominently displayed throughout the production area
- ❑ Promoted safe practices to subordinates on a regular basis
- ❑ Held safety drills in the department once a quarter
- ❑ Recognized subordinates who excelled at following safety guidelines
- ❑ Checked regularly that all emergency supplies were complete and operational
- ❑ Instructed subordinates in organizational safety regulations and procedures each week

❸ Met Standards (MS)

- ❑ Ensured that all production work was completed within safety guidelines
- ❑ Held a safety record of less than ____ accidents in the review period
- ❑ Reviewed organizational safety regulations and procedures with subordinates on a regular basis
- ❑ Adhered to all safe practices in own work
- ❑ Posted safety reminders and procedures for emergencies
- ❑ Followed all OSHA regulations and requirements
- ❑ Made safety training classes available to subordinates
- ❑ Tested safety equipment and inspected first aid boxes once each quarter

❷ Below Standards (BS)

- ❑ Had a record of ＿＿＿ accidents within his department in the review period
- ❑ Did not instruct subordinates in OSHA regulations and requirements, only posted them
- ❑ Posted safety reminders and procedures for emergencies only in restrooms
- ❑ Conducted safety training classes only when mandated by superiors
- ❑ Was cited for unsafe practices ＿＿＿ times in the review period
- ❑ Did not monitor for compliance among subordinates in wearing safety gear in areas where it's required
- ❑ Put production numbers above safety considerations

❶ Far Below Standards (FBS)

- ❑ Had a record of ＿＿＿ safety infractions in the review period
- ❑ Did not enforce the wearing of safety gear in areas that required it
- ❑ Had not updated safety and first aid posters in years
- ❑ Had ＿＿＿ OSHA infractions pending
- ❑ Did not use safe work practices
- ❑ Put production figures above everything else, including safety
- ❑ Neglected regular maintenance of equipment to keep it within the manufacturer's safe operation guidelines
- ❑ Did not ever check safety equipment or first aid supplies

❶ Not Observed (NO), Not Ratable (NR), Not Applicable (NA), Failed (F)

- ❑ Not observed
- ❑ Created a safety hazard for any employees within his area
- ❑ Did not demonstrate that he is qualified to serve in this position

- Review the recommendations at the end of this section (see page 171) and adapt those that apply.

- Review the employee's safety record and the areas where he needs to improve in detail, ask the employee for his response, and listen carefully.

- List each improvement the employee needs to make in the next quarter, such as these:

  - Enter organizational safety training and/or other lifesaving and first aid training programs immediately and pass with high grades.

  - Institute safety practices and the wearing of safety equipment immediately.

  - Check all equipment manuals for routine maintenance, and bring all procedures up to date: get in compliance with OSHA regulations and requirements and instruct subordinates.

  - Begin to put a new emphasis on safety and initiate a program to recognize and reward safe practices and recommendations for improved safety.

  - Restrict access to potentially dangerous areas, and make sure subordinates working in these areas regard safety as their number one priority.

  - Begin to require that subordinates take first aid and lifesaving emergency training.

  - Maintain all work tools in proper working condition.

  - Insist on a zero-tolerance policy for safety infractions.

- Have the employee write up his own personal plan for how he will improve his safety skills in the next quarter, being sure that he expresses these in specific terms, and schedule a meeting within the week to review the plan and have the employee sign it.

Self-Confidence

The feeling of conviction and assurance that comes from the employee's belief in his abilities, and of being capable of doing a task, is invaluable. Weight this quality in relationship to how it helps the employee perform his job.

⑤ Outstanding (O)
- ❑ Was fearless in taking on any task
- ❑ Possessed the calm assurance that she was capable of performing very well, no matter what the assignment
- ❑ Never hesitated to take a leadership role or take on new projects
- ❑ Sought opportunities to take on new areas of responsibility
- ❑ Volunteered for challenging assignments others were reluctant to grapple with
- ❑ Was quick to present new ideas and make suggestions in department meetings
- ❑ Offered solutions to difficult questions and made proposals for changes in procedures

④ Exceeded Standards (ES)
- ❑ Was willing to volunteer for assignments that others feared taking on
- ❑ Would take on a new challenging project if called on
- ❑ Offered new ideas and suggestions after he had done the necessary research
- ❑ Took a leadership role when asked
- ❑ Was not afraid to stand up in front of a meeting without preparation
- ❑ Led teams on _____ occasions
- ❑ Volunteered to be the face of the organization at several outside meetings

❸ Met Standards (MS)

- ❏ Volunteered occasionally after doing extensive research and building his platform
- ❏ Took on ____ challenging projects after study and preparation
- ❏ Received a rating of ____ from subordinates for his handling of instruction programs
- ❏ Was given a rating of ____ from the audience after his presentation in a meeting
- ❏ Did an "average" job in leadership as rated by coworkers
- ❏ Served as spokesperson for the department after being urged to do so by subordinates
- ❏ Led group discussions with a ____% success rate

❷ Below Standards (BS)

- ❏ Was reluctant to be high profile in any group meeting situation
- ❏ Turned down the opportunity to present at a meeting citing a lack of knowledge
- ❏ Did not volunteer to be team leader even when asked
- ❏ Shunned the spotlight
- ❏ Was tongue-tied when called on for any reason
- ❏ Questioned his judgment at every turn when asked to take the lead on a project
- ❏ Made repeated requests to make changes in his work even after it was turned in
- ❏ Failed to complete written assignments on deadline because he was still tinkering with the end report

❶ Far Below Standards (FBS)

- ❏ Was paralyzed if asked to take a leadership role
- ❏ Became physically ill when deadlines were looming or if asked to be team leader
- ❏ Questioned his judgment and needed others to reassure him of the direction to take

- ❑ Avoided any possible situation where he would have to be visible to coworkers or supervisors
- ❑ Would be absent if asked to present at a meeting
- ❑ Failed to take on a project solo when asked to do so

Ⓞ Not Observed (NO), Not Ratable (NR), Not Applicable (NA), Failed (F)
- ❑ Not observed
- ❑ Failed to show the required self-confidence to be able to function in this position

Recommended Action Steps for the Manager

- ▪ Review the recommendations at the end of this section (see page 171) and adapt all that apply.
- ▪ Tell the employee that he needs to increase his self-confidence in order to grow and advance in his career: be specific about how he might proceed, and use numbers and tasks or projects whenever possible, such as these:
  - — Make the decision to work on self-confidence.
  - — Take the step of contributing during meetings.
  - — Step up and take a leadership role.
  - — Review work thoroughly before submitting.
  - — Select a mentor and ask for help in areas where weak.

Strategic Thinking

The ability to critically examine and challenge the way things are done within the organization to come up with new and improved policies, plans, and prioritized goals—while identifying potential risks and opportunities—is a rare and useful skill. Weight it proportionately based on the role it has in the employee's job description.

❺ Outstanding (O)

- ❏ Developed long-term strategies (three to five years) based on expert analysis of strengths and weaknesses of the organization and the opportunities and threats in the marketplace
- ❏ Demonstrated the ability to produce realistic and achievable ideas
- ❏ Identified gaps between processes and procedures and operational tactics and was able to make adjustments to close those gaps
- ❏ Was able to match people to positions for maximum efficiency
- ❏ Possessed the ability to play out potential plans to see possible pitfalls as well as benefits
- ❏ Delivered excellent potential project budgets with an accuracy rate of ____%
- ❏ Saw profit opportunities unrecognized by coworkers or superiors
- ❏ Presented a complete picture of cost, profit, and obstacles for ideas he suggested, including informed cost analysis and profit potential contribution
- ❏ Challenged the status quo with revolutionary ideas
- ❏ Possessed extensive knowledge of the state of the art and trends in the industry
- ❏ Addressed skillfully the logistics, tactics, and strategic aspects of proposals
- ❏ Excelled in producing accurate models and forecasts

❹ Exceeded Standards (ES)

- ❏ Offered rational needs and benefits perspective to new proposals
- ❏ Had a good grasp on real-world markets for new product ideas
- ❏ Kept up to date on competitive products, methods, and operations, which helped in the analysis process
- ❏ Supplied dependable research on options, risks, and benefits
- ❏ Took a valuable long-term view of every proposal

- Played the role of devil's advocate skillfully and asked strategic questions in response to proposed ideas
- Used metric calculations to create budgets with ____% accuracy
- Was good at forecasting possible output and profits
- Brought a valuable management perspective to each idea

❸ Met Standards (MS)

- Offered comparative facts and figures of current operations with an accuracy rate of ____% to ____%
- Had an average grasp on industry standards and practices for useful reference
- Offered real-life production considerations, including costs, to new ideas suggested
- Was capable of adding to the strategic planning discussion with astute questions
- Provided dependable research on possible cost of proposals with ____% accuracy
- Produced models and forecasts with ____% accuracy
- Brought management views and considerations to the discussion

❷ Below Standards (BS)

- Contributed current operational cost factors to the discussion with only ____% accuracy rate
- Added infrequently to proposals with real-life production examples
- Needed assistance in supplying current cost-comparative figures
- Could not add value in the area of new trends and state-of-the-industry input
- Needed assistance in writing a comprehensive proposal
- Was incapable of producing models and forecasts that met the ____% accuracy standard
- Resisted new ideas and proposals
- Failed to research or think through ideas before offering them

❑ Needed help in drawing logical conclusions

❑ Did not project ideas into workable plans

❑ Lacked the ability to use metric systems that would be useful

① Far Below Standards (FBS)

❑ Had limited or no ability to add to strategic discussions

❑ Did not have a handle on current operational costs for comparative use

❑ Could not process an idea through to its possible operational impact

❑ Added no value to the strategic process

❑ Did not consider management impact of his ideas

❑ Created a negative influence in the strategic process

⓪ Not Observed (NO), Not Ratable (NR), Not Applicable (NA), Failed (F)

❑ Not applicable

❑ Was not capable of functioning in this role

Recommended Action Steps for the Manager

- Review the recommendations at the end of this section (see page 171) and include those that apply.

- List the incremental improvements the employee needs to make in the next quarter, such as these:

  – Develop a better knowledge of current organization operations, goals, and objectives.

  – Study the state of the art and future trends of the industry.

  – Learn as much as possible about competitive operations and new directions.

  – Gain in-depth knowledge of customer/client needs for the future.

Stress Tolerance

The ability to cope with and effectively manage psychological and emotional turmoil that may result from pressures within the workplace varies greatly from one employee to the next. And, of course, some jobs are much more pressure filled than others. Weight this skill proportionately based on the need for the employee to function at a high level under stress, without suffering anxiety or transferring pressure onto his coworkers and subordinates.

⑤ Outstanding (O)
- ❏ Anticipated and was prepared for stressful situations
- ❏ Adjusted to uncertainties and changes in the workplace while remaining composed
- ❏ Worked well in stressful situations
- ❏ Did not drop a beat in the heat of pressing deadlines
- ❏ Implemented positive measures to relieve the anxiety of subordinates
- ❏ Set a fine example for how to deal with stress
- ❏ Dissipated anxiety in subordinates by skillful use of management techniques
- ❏ Provided support for subordinates going through difficulties

④ Exceeded Standards (ES)
- ❏ Remained calm in crisis situations
- ❏ Took quick action when ____ work-related emergencies occurred and avoided compound crises
- ❏ Was able to absorb the unreasonable demands of superiors while remaining calm
- ❏ Righted the ship with minimum disruption to the ongoing work process when emergencies occurred
- ❏ Handled ____ crises without the need for extraordinary measures

- ❏ Held a reputation as a good listener for subordinates undergoing stress
- ❏ Managed ____ demands from superiors and subordinates effectively
- ❏ Refused to get rattled by unscheduled events and crisis situations
- ❏ Set a good example of how to deal with stress

❸ Met Standards (MS)

- ❏ Was usually capable of handling pressure from superiors without emotionally reacting
- ❏ Remained calm in ____% of stressful situations
- ❏ Used organizational resources like HR for help in dealing with subordinates experiencing emotional problems
- ❏ Called on coworkers for help when departmental stresses increased
- ❏ Handled ____ crises during the review period by using extraordinary measures
- ❏ Coped adequately with uncomfortable situations
- ❏ Served as an intermediary for subordinates who went to her for help, and referred them to HR for counseling
- ❏ Was able to multitask and keep several deadlines and targets proceeding on schedule
- ❏ Showed a good resistance to annoyance
- ❏ Was seldom upset by changes in scheduling

❷ Below Standards (BS)

- ❏ Showed signs of stress when scheduling demands changed
- ❏ Was not able to handle ____ crises that occurred at the same time without intervention by superiors
- ❏ Coped with ____ uncomfortable situations only after supervisor stepped in to intercede
- ❏ Met changing demands by having a tantrum
- ❏ Refused to hear the complaints of subordinates who were experiencing stress

- Responded to subordinates under stress by telling them it's part of the job, and if they can't handle it, they should resign
- Called on coworkers to bail him out of stressful situations ____ times during the review period
- Shut down if ____ conflicting directives were given
- Needed hand-holding during stressful situations

❶ Far Below Standards (FBS)

- Buckled when ____ simultaneous crises occurred
- Could only adequately cope with a single deadline at a time
- Was myopic in focus and could not meet the demands of this position
- Blew up when deadlines were changed
- Was sent into turmoil when there was a need for a scheduling change
- Would not discuss emotional matters with subordinates
- Showed complete intolerance for competing priorities
- Could not change course when the situation required it
- Made sure everyone in his work area suffered if he was experiencing stress
- Was incapable of civility when under pressure

❶ Not Observed (NO), Not Ratable (NR), Not Applicable (NA), Failed (F)

- Not capable of handling the varied and multiple stresses of this position
- Not observed
- Not applicable

Recommended Action Steps for the Manager

- Review the recommendations at the end of this section (see page 171) and include those that apply.
- Examine with the employee his record for handling stress over the review period. Use real numbers and examples from the details

you have in your employee journal, and then ask for the employee's response and input.

- Continue to develop the employee's ability to handle stress and state the areas where the employee needs to improve, such as these:
  - Learn to plan better for possible changes in scheduling.
  - Control emotional outbursts in the workplace.
  - Master the ability to be flexible in meeting changing demands.
  - Set a good example for subordinates in how to handle stress.
  - Develop the ability to multitask and remain calm.
  - Tune in to the emotional distress of subordinates and coworkers and learn to listen effectively and offer help.
- Ask the employee to write up his own personal plan for improvement and development in this skill area in the next quarter, and schedule a meeting to review the plan.

Supervisory and Staff Development Skills

There are many skills required in order to monitor, manage, and develop subordinates' work skills. Duties may include effective hiring, training, disciplining, promoting, rewarding, and other activities. Weight this skill area according to the employee's responsibility to fulfill these duties.

⑤ Outstanding (O)
- ❑ Demonstrated a profound dedication and sensitivity to the needs of subordinates
- ❑ Was highly respected by subordinates and coworkers
- ❑ Led subordinates by setting an excellent example
- ❑ Allowed subordinates adequate time and freedom to ask questions and give input
- ❑ Had complete knowledge of the job skills required by subordinates

- Was a very capable instructor and able to teach subordinates superior skills
- Gave subordinates great feedback on a regular basis
- Developed effective incentive programs for subordinates
- Kept abreast of subordinates' career goals, and connected them with programs that would benefit them in reaching their goals
- Encouraged subordinates to continue to develop, even when it meant he would lose them
- Served as an effective mentor to subordinates
- Interceded for his subordinates with all organization departments and personnel
- Was held in the highest esteem by subordinates
- Created an accepting and safe environment in which subordinates were not afraid to make errors while learning
- Used recognition, reward, and award programs effectively to develop subordinates
- Looked for new ways to help develop subordinates' skills
- Controlled work flow and balanced staffing to prevent over- and under-staffing demands
- Brought out the best in subordinates

❹ Exceeded Standards (ES)

- Used supervisory techniques skillfully
- Gave clear and definitive instructions to subordinates
- Controlled work flow and job assignments
- Received marks of ____ to ____ from subordinates for approachability
- Set expectations high but also inspired subordinates to do their best
- Counseled subordinates in ways that would help them develop and reach their career goals
- Motivated subordinates and coworkers to reach department and personal goals

- ❏ Allowed subordinates to take on challenging projects
- ❏ Listened effectively to subordinate input ____% of the time
- ❏ Knew the capabilities of subordinates fairly well
- ❏ Defended subordinates to other organization departments
- ❏ Had the loyalty of subordinates

❸ Met Standards (MS)

- ❏ Ranked at ____% in subordinates' training rating
- ❏ Used the organization's recognition and rewards program to incentivize subordinates
- ❏ Ran training programs for subordinates on a regular basis
- ❏ Was rated at ____% to ____% in controlling work flow and setting deadlines and targets for subordinates
- ❏ Restricted new assignments to those subordinates with mastery of skills test scores
- ❏ Asked for input from subordinates during staff meetings each week
- ❏ Received "good" ratings from subordinates in approachability and listening skills
- ❏ Was rated "good" in goal setting for work output
- ❏ Communicated with supervisors and related departments satisfactorily

❷ Below Standards (BS)

- ❏ Did not initiate communication with subordinates and was defensive when approached
- ❏ Was considered aloof and detached by subordinates
- ❏ Curtailed subordinates' input and responses on a regular basis
- ❏ Needed assistance in controlling workflow to avoid routine overload situations
- ❏ Left subordinates in the dark about work assignments and development possibilities

- Blamed subordinates, rather than defending them, to other departments
- Did not develop a team spirit among staff
- Did not create training, mentoring, or promotional opportunities for his subordinates
- Was close-minded in approach to work processes
- Seemed unable or unwilling to delegate
- Lacked confidence in subordinates' capabilities
- Failed to call in outside help, even when it was apparent he needed it

❶ Far Below Standards (FBS)

- Believed information is power and did not share with subordinates
- Had an arrogant attitude and was completely unapproachable
- Was unwilling to discuss personal goals and career development with subordinates
- Criticized openly and belittled subordinates _____ times in front of others
- Lost her temper with little provocation
- Demonstrated only a command-and-demand style of management
- Failed to keep current on subordinates' performance reviews
- Had _____ grievances filed by subordinates during the review period
- Refused to delegate or allow subordinates to take any leadership role
- Did not use any of the organizational recognition, reward, or award programs with his subordinates

❷ Not Observed (NO), Not Ratable (NR), Not Applicable (NA), Failed (F)

- Did not demonstrate that he is capable of handling the demands of this position
- Not observed
- Failed

Recommended Action Steps for the Manager

- Review the recommendations at the end of this section (see page 171) and adapt all those that apply.

- Suggest that the employee consider all of these action steps that apply:

  - Apologize to subordinates for specific grievances where they exist, and pledge to make the appropriate changes to create a welcoming and positive work environment.

  - Ask subordinates for their input (which may be offered anonymously) on ways the work environment can be improved.

  - Improve the planning and scheduling of work to address subordinate overload.

  - Eliminate the negativity in the relationship with subordinates.

  - Enroll in anger management and other appropriate classes to improve interpersonal relationships with subordinates.

  - Institute programs of recognition and awards for subordinates' outstanding performance.

  - Begin a program of cross-training and substitution within the work area to more effectively and efficiently handle production.

  - Announce to subordinates that a "new day has dawned," and the employee will begin to better fulfill his role as supervisor and staff developer.

  - Set up meetings with individual subordinates to begin to relate better.

- Ask the employee to write up his personal plan for the immediate future and address how he will improve his performance (especially in deficit areas) in the next quarter. Schedule a meeting to review this plan with the employee and give your feedback within the next week.

Tactfulness

Being sensitive to the feelings of others, and adroit in managing interpersonal relations in a way that avoids offense can be a challenge in the workplace. This is a skill every employee needs to master in order to make business go well. Weight it accordingly.

❺ Outstanding (O)

- ❑ Scored very high in ability to handle difficult situations
- ❑ Negotiated conflicts between subordinates with great skill
- ❑ Was able to say no without offending
- ❑ Followed proper protocol every time
- ❑ Interceded and left both sides of a conflict feeling satisfied that the issue was resolved
- ❑ Conveyed appreciation and respect to everyone equally
- ❑ Possessed both grace and style in making presentations
- ❑ Mediated with wisdom
- ❑ Disagreed with respect and without offending
- ❑ Refused to become combative when provoked
- ❑ Admitted errors tactfully
- ❑ Used proper etiquette in all situations

❹ Exceeded Standards (ES)

- ❑ Was cordial but firm in her position
- ❑ Did not let confrontations throw him
- ❑ Avoided arguments by diffusing them
- ❑ Accepted criticism graciously, even when it was unfounded
- ❑ Was diplomatic in correcting the mistakes of others
- ❑ Tried to reach mutual agreement without offending
- ❑ Could say no without offending ____% of the time

- ❑ Was successful in restoring calm when a conflict arose
- ❑ Served as a mediator when coworkers had a conflict

❸ Met Standards (MS)
- ❑ Could say no effectively ____% of the time
- ❑ Did not take sides in an argument
- ❑ Had the ability to mediate conflicts ____% of the time
- ❑ Referred disputes between subordinates to HR when he could not mediate them
- ❑ Was firm and decisive in resolving conflicts ____% of the time
- ❑ Had a good grasp of proper etiquette in the workplace
- ❑ Accepted constructive criticism without anger ____% of the time
- ❑ Was usually unflappable during a conflict

❷ Below Standards (BS)
- ❑ Took sides during subordinates' disputes
- ❑ Had trouble saying no tactfully
- ❑ Was unable to mediate most disputes
- ❑ Could not receive constructive criticism without anger
- ❑ Did not demonstrate basic knowledge of proper etiquette for the workplace
- ❑ Got rattled and angry when conflicts occurred
- ❑ Blundered in presentations to customers and visitors
- ❑ Used off-color and offensive language routinely

❶ Far Below Standards (FBS)
- ❑ Could not fill a role as mediator for subordinates
- ❑ Had an offensive manner that exacerbated conflicts
- ❑ Lacked the ability to be firm in stating a position
- ❑ Leaked personal information learned in confidence on ____ occasions

❑ Failed to use even the most basic proper etiquette on ____ occasions

❑ Caused a disturbance where there was calm

❑ Offended customers and visitors on ____ occasions

⓪ Not Observed (NO), Not Ratable (NR), Not Applicable (NA), Failed (F)

❑ Failed in ___ situations to properly handle subordinate conflicts

❑ Responded in entirely inappropriate manner to subordinates on ____ occasions

❑ Not observed

❑ Cannot fulfill the requirements for this skill in this position

Recommended Action Steps for the Manager

■ Review the recommendations at the end of this section (see page 171) and include all those that apply.

■ Make additional suggestions as appropriate:

— Learn to listen effectively to subordinate complaints.

— Intercede in conflicts between subordinates when a problem arises; don't let it fester.

— Learn the basic rules of proper business etiquette. Increase ability to keep personnel and personal information confidential.

— Be discreet in handling all disciplinary matters.

— Start with a positive statement and follow it with a logical reason for declining when saying no.

Teamwork

Getting along with others and working in a cohesive and harmonious way to accomplish a common goal is an essential skill for almost every employee. Although it is measured as part of other personal skills, you may want to include it in your performance review since it can be the sole basis for an overall positive or negative evaluation.

❺ Outstanding (O)

- ❏ Put the value of teamwork above personal considerations
- ❏ Fostered team building and cooperation with coworkers and subordinates
- ❏ Had an exceptional ability to put the right combination of subordinates together on each team
- ❏ Did not tolerate schisms within the teams
- ❏ Brought out the best in individuals in the roles he assigned to them on teams
- ❏ Was always available to coach teams to a higher level of achievement
- ❏ Created unique team bonuses, rewards, and recognition programs that motivated teams
- ❏ Promoted a united front to other departments, even when teams had conflicts
- ❏ Resolved team issues quickly and easily
- ❏ Conducted effective team meetings
- ❏ Had the attitude that what conflicts originate within the team get settled there for the sake of the team
- ❏ Focused teams on organizational goals and objectives
- ❏ Encouraged participation of all team members
- ❏ Completed all team assignments on time and with exceptional results

❹ Exceeded Standards (ES)

- ❏ Was a very good team builder
- ❏ Participated on ____ teams during the review period with good results
- ❏ Promoted dismissing individual considerations in favor of team success
- ❏ Encouraged participation in team meetings by all members
- ❏ Insisted on mutual respect for and by all team members

- ❏ Did not let team members coast without making their own contribution
- ❏ Worked well with all other team members
- ❏ Made sure all team members kept each other informed about project status and changes

❸ Met Standards (MS)

- ❏ Was a good team member and worked hard to deliver consistent with the team goals
- ❏ Kept a positive attitude, even in the face of other team members not performing up to standard
- ❏ Focused on the team goals and did not let obstacles and changes frustrate him
- ❏ Made a consistent contribution to the team effort
- ❏ Was rated "good" by team members for attention to assignment details, delivery dates, and output
- ❏ Served on ____ teams during the review period with positive results
- ❏ Had a record of showing respect and dignity to all team members
- ❏ Added to the team spirit and camaraderie by his positive input
- ❏ Was chosen for possible team assignments ____ times during the review period

❷ Below Standards (BS)

- ❏ Had to be reminded by the team leader what the assignment was and when to deliver it
- ❏ Was late with his contribution ____ times in the review period
- ❏ Produced results that did not match the assignment given
- ❏ Was prone to negative comments and input, which cast a pall over the entire team
- ❏ Was only asked to serve on a team ____ time(s) during the review period because of his reputation as an undercontributor

❑ Preferred to work alone and resisted team assignments

❑ Did not interact or share with other team members as required

❑ Missed ____ deadlines for team contribution during the review period

❑ Was prone to shoot down other team members' ideas or dismiss them out of hand

❑ Was rated at ____% for team participation by other team members

❑ Craved personal recognition above team recognition

❶ Far Below Standards (FBS)

❑ Destroyed team spirit with disruptive behavior and negative comments, wasting the time and energy of other team members

❑ Received ____ complaints by team members who refused to work with him in the future

❑ Shared personal information that had been given to her by other team members in confidence

❑ Failed to do team assignment

❑ Refused to take an assignment

❑ Lost his temper during team meetings

❑ Insisted on controlling the team, even though he was not the captain

❑ Received a ____% acceptable rating from other team members for performance and contribution

❶ Not Observed (NO), Not Ratable (NR), Not Applicable (NA), Failed (F)

❑ Not observed

❑ Failed to make a team contribution

❑ Not applicable

Recommended Action Steps for the Manager

■ Review the recommendations at the end of this section (see page 171) and adapt all those that apply.

■ Tell the employee precisely what needs to be improved in this skill area for him to continue to develop his career, be promoted, and grow. Here are some suggestions the manager might give to the employee:

— Improve your listening skills by ___% in the next quarter.

— Eliminate arguing from your team participation communication.

— Increase your positive team contribution by ___% in the next quarter.

— Take a team leadership role.

— Improve your on-time team-task record by ___% in the next quarter.

— Monitor team progress and check with members to keep them on target and on deadline.

— Keep all personal information shared inside the team confidential.

Technical Skills

The employee who has the precise technical skills required to accomplish the specific tasks described in his job description is well on his way to job mastery. Weight this skill category to reflect that value.

❺ Outstanding (O)

❑ Mastered all work procedures and processes

❑ Taught coworkers and subordinates new methods and procedures to shortcut workload

❑ Possessed highly specialized skills in software applications

❑ Kept informed on state-of-the-art and new technology trends in the field

❑ Went far beyond the job description in checking and double-checking technical results

❑ Innovated and developed new methods and tools for improving speed and accuracy of output

- Made sure subordinates' skills were up to date and certification was current
- Adapted extremely well to changes in technology and new procedure requirements
- Maintained excellent records and wrote comprehensive reports
- Documented all changes with written procedures for others to follow
- Was the go-to person for anyone in the organization who had a technical problem
- Was able to translate own knowledge into the organization's vision for the future

❹ Exceeded Standards (ES)

- Was rated _____ out of a possible _____ in knowledge of technical procedures by subordinates
- Taught coworkers and subordinates new methodologies and procedures as they became available
- Stayed current on emerging technologies and was able to envision how to use them to improve organizational results
- Knew how to expertly use the tools of this position
- Had a good knowledge of software products and applications
- Received a rating of _____ % by coworkers for his ability and willingness to help them solve their technical issues
- Documented new procedures and practices and wrote reports with _____% accuracy
- Held a record of _____ new and useful technologies introduced in the review period that increased output by _____% and reduced errors by _____%
- Assisted subordinates in maintaining up-to-date certification and continuing education training
- Considered thoroughly the organizational impact of new technologies before recommending acquisition
- Could translate new technologies into profitable application outcomes

❸ Met Standards (MS)

- ❏ Knew how to use the technical tools and methodologies required for this position

- ❏ Kept certification dates of his subordinates firmly in mind and notified subordinates of the need to update

- ❏ Taught subordinates basic new technologies as needed ____% of the time

- ❏ Learned new technologies required for the position within the required time period

- ❏ Fixed many routine technical problems and had resources to call on for fixing others

- ❏ Kept up to date on procedural changes required for job performance

- ❏ Wrote procedures and reports at an acceptable level

- ❏ Coordinated with coworkers on technical advances applicable to their needs

❷ Below Standards (BS)

- ❏ Lagged behind the curve in the adoption of the latest technologies needed to update procedures

- ❏ Needed to be retrained in ____ job skills to meet the new requirements of the job

- ❏ Failed to translate his work to system-wide applications ____% of the time

- ❏ Allowed his and subordinates' certifications to lapse

- ❏ Did not keep equipment updated with the latest applications

- ❏ Did not participate in continuing education classes to keep current on new technologies

- ❏ Did not take the required steps to change over to "paperless" office procedures as mandated

- ❏ Could not diagnose and fix the equipment required for his job

- ❏ Did not document procedures and processes with written reports

- Lacked the knowledge to use the latest and best software applications
- Rated ____% in mastery of the new equipment

❶ Far Below Standards (FBS)

- Did not demonstrate adequate training to be able to function in this job
- Had expired certification and had not taken steps to update it
- Showed no interest in learning new and necessary software applications
- Did not document procedures and processes as required
- Failed to do routine maintenance of his equipment or install new software products ____ times during the review period
- Resisted ____ attempts to retrain him in the required skills during the review period
- Did not have an adequate knowledge of the basic procedures and processes required to perform his job

❶ Not Observed (NO), Not Ratable (NR), Not Applicable (NA), Failed (F)

- Not observed
- Not applicable
- Failed to meet the minimum technical requirements of this position

Recommended Action Steps for the Manager

- Review the recommendations at the end of this section (see page 171) and adapt all that apply.
- Tell the employee what needs to be improved in this skills area for him to continue to develop to meet his career goals and/or be promoted; here are some suggestions you may want to include:
  - Embrace new technologies that are required to perform this job.
  - Sign up for the next continuing education class to bring certification current.

- Agree to participate in in-service or community training programs to update technical skills.
- Begin to get current on changing technologies in the industry.
- Initiate a program of equipment maintenance and updating to be done each month.
- Complete new equipment training within the next month.
- Begin a daily routine of record keeping that documents procedures and processes.
- Train subordinates in technology skills in which they are deficient.

Time Management

Excelling in this skill requires properly allocating time to accomplish competing demands of a job. It requires budgeting time effectively. It's very important to every job and should be weighted to reflect that fact.

❺ Outstanding (O)
- ❏ Used an expert system of analyzing the amount of time needed for each requirement of his job and improved on times consistently
- ❏ Prized efficient use of time as his most important function and did it very well
- ❏ Rewarded subordinates who came up with time-saving procedures
- ❏ Emphasized effective time management to his coworkers and subordinates and led by example
- ❏ Was expert at budgeting time requirements to do procedures properly
- ❏ Managed to always get work done well, regardless of interruptions and obstacles

- ❑ Kept a schedule of duties and time allocations for the department to make sure deadlines were met
- ❑ Was rated at ____% to ____% accurate on estimating labor requirements for client proposals
- ❑ Arrived at work early, started on time, and required subordinates to start on time
- ❑ Never missed a deadline or delivered a project that didn't meet the requirements
- ❑ Maintained production schedule, even when interruptions and slowdowns occurred

❹ Exceeded Standards (ES)

- ❑ Anticipated slowdowns and interruptions well and was ready with alternatives to keep production on target
- ❑ Used contingency planning well to make sure work was done on deadline
- ❑ Budgeted time effectively to make sure schedules were met
- ❑ Did not allow time wasting within the department
- ❑ Led by example, arriving at work on time ____% of the time, and starting work by ____
- ❑ Had a record of delivering on deadline ____% of the time
- ❑ Notified clients of delays and unanticipated problems ____% of the time and then delivered on time
- ❑ Overcame delays and interruptions well to keep projects on schedule ____% of the time
- ❑ Prioritized well
- ❑ Managed time well and finished work on time
- ❑ Worked steadily and efficiently and didn't procrastinate
- ❑ Created a productive work atmosphere for subordinates

❸ Met Standards (MS)

- ❏ Prioritized so that all work processes proceeded on schedule
- ❏ Was able to manage multiple tasks and interruptions and still keep work on schedule ____% of the time
- ❏ Did not allow subordinates to waste time or create distractions
- ❏ Kept deadlines firmly in mind and had a record of meeting them ____% of the time
- ❏ Estimated task completion times with ____% accuracy
- ❏ Computed labor time estimates for proposals with ____% accuracy
- ❏ Used time management tools with ____% proficiency
- ❏ Delegated effectively ____% of the time
- ❏ Did not overpromise on delivery dates or output
- ❏ Coordinated schedules with coworkers to make sure all departments were working together to meet the organization's goals
- ❏ Arrived at work on time and began work on time ____% of the time

❷ Below Standards (BS)

- ❏ Had a record of being more than ____ late with delivery ____% of the time
- ❏ Failed to coordinate with coworkers, producing interdepartmental slowdowns or work stoppage ____ times during the review period
- ❏ Underestimated labor figures ____ times by ____% to ____% during the review period
- ❏ Failed to arrive and start work on time ____% of the time; and started work on time only ____% of the time during the review period
- ❏ Allowed subordinates to come and go from the area at will and did not enforce time delivery deadlines ____% of the time
- ❏ Used time management tools at a proficiency rate of ____%
- ❏ Did not have a good handle on prioritizing and controlling interruptions
- ❏ Demonstrated the need to be retrained in time management techniques

- ❑ Overpromised on delivery ____% of the time, which eroded client confidence and lost the organization business
- ❑ Did not delegate well ____% of the time
- ❑ Got rattled and made errors when deadlines approached

❶ Far Below Standards (FBS)

- ❑ Had a record for the review period of not meeting deadlines ____% of the time
- ❑ Procrastinated ____ times on project completion during the review period
- ❑ Underestimated labor figures ____ times by ____% to ____% during the review period
- ❑ Was unable to manage interruptions and continue working
- ❑ Allowed subordinates to waste time and failed to meet deadlines ____% of the time during the review period
- ❑ Did not maintain an online production schedule or a written day planner schedule
- ❑ Did not delegate adequately under stress
- ❑ Got completely rattled and unable to continue work when deadlines approached
- ❑ Did not demonstrate the proper aptitude or skills to fill this position without extensive retraining

❶ Not Observed (NO), Not Ratable (NR), Not Applicable (NA), Failed (F)

- ❑ Not observed
- ❑ Not ratable
- ❑ Failed to meet any of the specifics of his job description

Recommended Action Steps for the Manager

- ■ Review the recommendations at the end of this section (see page 171) and adapt those that apply.
- ■ Make additional suggestions as appropriate:
  - – Increase on-time production by ____% in the next quarter.

- Learn to use the organization's time management tools with
  ___% proficiency.
- Agree to a mentorship with another employee in order to learn
  how to manage subordinates' output more effectively.
- Take in-service or community training or a course on time-
  management techniques.
- Perform a time study of subordinates' work and streamline
  processes for efficiency.
- Eliminate unnecessary interruptions.

- Ask the employee to write up his specific personal plan for
  improving in this area in the next quarter and schedule a meeting to
  review his plan.

More Recommended Action Steps for the Manager

The wise manager assesses the precise needs of each of his employees and coaches them to improve performance, and meet their developmental career goals. Here are some recommended steps that can work to help achieve this (Also review the specific recommendations listed after each core competency being evaluated.) Select and use those that you can adapt for each deficient personal skill area, and be sure to include them at the conclusion of the performance review during the "goals" phase.

- Review, precisely, the employee's performance, starting
  with the positive points and then cover the areas where the
  employee can, and needs to, improve. Be specific and supply
  actual numbers and examples from your employee journal
  and other organizational records whenever possible.

- Review in detail with the employee his deficiencies over the
  review period.

- Ask the employee to give his response and input concerning the areas of deficiency, and listen carefully for clues about measures you can recommend to help him improve in each area.

- Tell the employee how much improvement he must make and the time frame for that improvement.

- Ask the employee to re-state and commit to achieving the plan you have outlined.

- Consider arranging a mentorship for the employee with another employee within the organization who excels in the areas where the employee is deficient.

- Cycle the employee through the organization's policies, procedures, and values training—more than once, if need be.

- Ask the employee to write up a plan for how he will improve his performance and/or increase his skill level, review the plan with him, and connect him to any programs or classes that will help him develop in each precise deficient area. Have him sign the approved plan.

- Review with the employee specific organizational policies, procedures, and values and how they need to inform his conduct.

- Present training and educational course options that the employee may use to help build her skills.

- Inform the employee of how important it is to master the precise deficient skill and the career paths open to those who do.

- Require that the employee bring up to date any licenses, certificates, or other skills required to perform in his present job.

- Present to the employee the areas where improvement can be made, and cover the relevant areas where there are opportunities for additional development and promotion. List any support programs, mentorships, and training programs—inside and outside the organization—that will help the employee reach his goals.

- State exactly the levels of improvement the employee needs to achieve in the next quarter.

- Review all organizational policies and procedures with the employee and use examples of their application from his experience to illustrate the proper course of action.

The Job Skills/Performance Evaluation by Job Title and Function

EVERY ORGANIZATION writes employee job descriptions according to their specific needs, but there is a common skill set. Select from the lists the skills that apply to the employee you are reviewing. Use the employee's job description as the basis against which to measure performance. And be sure to keep job descriptions updated to reflect changes in duties and responsibilities.

From the skills you select, rate the employee's performance with the grading number that expresses his actual performance level (see page 6).

Accounting and Finance

Accountant/Bookkeeper

- ❑ Initiated, organized, and operated the organization's system software, online spreadsheets, and databases
- ❑ Produced reports with an accuracy rate of ____% to ____% in the review period
- ❑ Responded to requests for financial status updates immediately and accurately
- ❑ Delivered special summaries and analyses for the review period
- ❑ Projected income and cost factors
- ❑ Answered questions on financial statements in language that department heads could understand
- ❑ Was proactive in bringing financial issues to the proper administrator's attention
- ❑ Delivered monthly and quarterly financial reports by the deadline
- ❑ Ran a very efficient accounting department
- ❑ Demonstrated superior skills in financial research and reporting
- ❑ Kept the departmental accounting report procedures accurate and on time

Auditor

- ❑ Went beyond the numbers to interpret the organization's operation
- ❑ Kept department heads up to date on what their input meant
- ❑ Gave managers realistic feedback on possible outcomes of managerial plans
- ❑ Was proactive in raising financial issues considerations
- ❑ Studied all relevant regulations and upcoming requirements and alerted management

- ❏ Researched possible impact of proposals, saving the organization money by warning against potentially unprofitable ones
- ❏ Delivered precise and accurate audits
- ❏ Was proactive in setting up ongoing audit controls to catch problems early
- ❏ Stayed current on regulations affecting the organization and instructed in ways to comply
- ❏ Explained audit results to managers' satisfaction
- ❏ Suggested a plan for creating controls to eliminate future problems early
- ❏ Kept department heads informed ____% of the time during the review period

Financial Analyst

- ❏ Provided management with excellent proposals for organizational investments
- ❏ Completed financial forecasts with ____% accuracy
- ❏ Oversaw all financial reporting procedures in a timely and accurate manner
- ❏ Completed budgets and forecasts as directed by management with ____% accuracy
- ❏ Produced profits on investments of ____% to ____% consistently
- ❏ Used spreadsheets, graphs, and charts to make financials understandable to all levels of employees
- ❏ Interpreted yield, stability, future trends, and economic influences consistently and accurately
- ❏ Stayed ahead of the curve on industry trends and economic growth opportunities
- ❏ Used trends knowledge to identify new product proposals

Financial Manager/Credit and Collections Manager

- ❑ Created a comprehensive plan for organizational profitability
- ❑ Balanced cash flow and expenditures expertly
- ❑ Handled collections with both skill and delicacy
- ❑ Collected ____% of all delinquent invoices and accounts
- ❑ Retained ____% of delinquent customers
- ❑ Supervised staff with ratings of "good" to "excellent"
- ❑ Developed effective collection procedures
- ❑ Had an outstanding record of success in extending credit to worthy customers
- ❑ Managed credit line and credit extensions for the organization without glitches
- ❑ Reduced bad debt write-offs by ____% using effective collection procedures
- ❑ Set customer credit limits within organizational policy
- ❑ Kept customer credit histories complete and up to date
- ❑ Processed credit applications within ____ days of submission
- ❑ Updated customer credit histories each quarter
- ❑ Supervised collection subordinates with "excellent" ratings by the majority

Banks, Credit Unions, Mortgage Companies, and Financial Institutions

Bank Manager

- ❑ Oversaw all the sales of the bank
- ❑ Handled daily operations of the bank in a manner that created a friendly and efficient environment
- ❑ Managed and instituted systems for checks and balances to avoid customer banking errors

- ❏ Kept the bank operating at a profitability rate of ____%
- ❏ Developed ____ programs to increase customer base
- ❏ Supervised all the employees with ratings of "good" to "excellent"
- ❏ Was able to handle, without errors, the many functions required of the operation

Customer Service Representative

- ❏ Was the friendly face of the bank; created a great first impression
- ❏ Mastered complete knowledge of bank systems, customer banking vehicles, and procedures
- ❏ Was quick to diagnose customer needs and come up with the best banking solutions
- ❏ Communicated banking solutions to customers in terms they could easily understand
- ❏ Handled ____% of customer questions and quickly referred others to the right personnel
- ❏ Sold existing customers ____ new banking services and products during the review period
- ❏ Kept her cool and calmed customers ____% of the time, including the angriest customers
- ❏ Handled money without making errors ____% of the time
- ❏ Worked quickly and efficiently to process customers and minimize wait times

Loan Officer

- ❏ Was responsible for researching and collecting data, evaluating, authorizing, or recommending approval of loan applications for customers or businesses
- ❏ Approved ____ loans during the review period with ____% success rate
- ❏ Completed exhaustive research to qualify credit-worthy loan applicants and eliminate risky applicants

- Handled details of customers' loan applications expertly, following up as necessary with all details
- Initiated, processed, and opened loans to businesses
- Collected loan overdue payments
- Received "very helpful" ratings from all loan customers with whom he worked
- Conveyed bank loan vehicle programs and details to customers
- Completed ____ cold calls on businesses and developed loan prospects
- Processed pending loan applications, including collection of missing details and follow-up with customers
- Kept loan customers informed of their loan applications status, and answered all their questions about bank policies and procedures with "satisfactory" or better ratings
- Processed ____ loan applications within the promised ____ time frame

Teller

- Handled large and small amounts of cash expertly
- Showed great attention to detail in making sure customers were satisfied
- Transferred funds between customer accounts without errors ____% of the time
- Balanced his cash drawer at the end of each day without shortage or extra funds ____% of the time

Construction

Carpenter

- Employed the sound rule of "measure twice, cut once" to ensure his work quality
- Had comprehensive knowledge of woodworking equipment and tools
- Complied with all safety rules and regulations

- ❏ Came up with superior solutions to a variety of construction problems
- ❏ Reduced materials waste on the job by ____% by using care and caution in materials storage
- ❏ Was able to measure and size accurately every time
- ❏ Brought his up-to-date knowledge of building codes and regulations to each project and saved the company work delays and possible fines and violations
- ❏ Performed each job on time and proficiently
- ❏ Showed high skill levels in building stairs, floors, and working with concrete
- ❏ Framed walls and installed trim without wasting materials
- ❏ Demonstrated a cooperative attitude and good work ethic

Estimator

- ❏ Prepared ____ cost estimates out of ____ total that came in with a ____% profit margin, right on target
- ❏ Was able to foresee hidden costs and alert management about special considerations
- ❏ Planned and allowed for contingencies in a cost-effective way
- ❏ Advised management about possible complications of potential projects and recommended against submitting a bid on problem projects
- ❏ Exhibited in-depth knowledge of reading construction plans, blueprints, and other construction specifications
- ❏ Had complete knowledge of local codes and regulations and used that knowledge well in creating bids
- ❏ Created budgets that were consistently within ____% to ____% accurate
- ❏ Displayed a strong knowledge of building science and construction processes, and employed both in creating his estimates
- ❏ Was certified in cost engineering and cost estimating and analysis

- ❏ Specified the use of the latest and best building materials and procedures
- ❏ Possessed strong knowledge of HVAC, electrical systems, and all relevant codes
- ❏ Worked well with all potential suppliers, developers, and managers
- ❏ Was skilled in using computerized software construction estimating spreadsheet programs, and sending, receiving, and attaching large drawing files using email or file transfer programs
- ❏ Displayed skill in using construction scheduling software

Foreman

- ❏ Managed ____ construction projects that came in ____% under budget for labor costs
- ❏ Received ratings of "good" to "excellent" from subordinates for his management style
- ❏ Reduced materials waste on the job by securing materials and training subordinates in specialized skills
- ❏ Increased profits by reducing redo labor costs with implementation of bonus and incentive programs for subordinates
- ❏ Managed and coordinated with subcontractors to avoid on-site conflicts and downtime by fine-tuning schedules and completing work on time
- ❏ Hired qualified new workers and carpenters
- ❏ Retained ____% of subordinates; had a turnover rate of ____%
- ❏ Planned carefully and scheduled with precision to ensure on-time supply deliveries
- ❏ Communicated with and conducted inspections by engineers, architects, and owners to ensure the project was approved at every stage
- ❏ Worked effectively with all levels of management and outside professionals and owners
- ❏ Enforced that use of proper safety gear and proper procedures were observed at all times

Laborer/Construction Worker

- ❑ Showed eagerness, speed, and efficiency in doing each task
- ❑ Listened and asked questions of supervisor(s) to understand the task completely
- ❑ Complied with all safety regulations
- ❑ Was capable of handling proficiently a variety of power tools, including nail guns, small mechanical hoists, measuring equipment, air hammers, cement mixers, and surveying equipment
- ❑ Kept all hand tools in good and safe working order
- ❑ Performed construction site preparation and cleanup completely, safely, neatly, and by the deadline
- ❑ Was willing and capable of taking on any task assigned, including setting up scaffolding, digging holes, mixing concrete, unloading trucks, hauling materials, and installing drywall

Engineering

Engineer/Principal Engineer

- ❑ Used professional engineering skills to complete and oversee all engineering projects with a ____% accuracy rate
- ❑ Completed all projects within ____ days of projected deadlines
- ❑ Conceptualized initial design specifications for ____ projects to submit to management for consideration
- ❑ Completed all engineering design drawings, schematics, and layouts as required
- ❑ Worked well with ____ departments to establish customer requirements, project cost factors, and estimate and allocate resources
- ❑ Supervised all work on ____ approved designs
- ❑ Estimated costs and time for design development with ____% accuracy

- ❏ Documented all work done and submitted timely progress reports to management
- ❏ Kept projects on budget by using cost-cutting measures whenever possible
- ❏ Ensured that off-site projects were maintained safely and completed accurately and in accordance with organizational policies and procedures
- ❏ Purchased all necessary materials and equipment to complete projects
- ❏ Hired staff members and retained ____% of his subordinates
- ❏ Secured approvals for changes during work on projects from management
- ❏ Enforced strict adherence to safety regulations at all times

Engineering Technician

- ❏ Conducted ____ tests on prototypes, new circuit designs, and/or transportation systems
- ❏ Assisted engineers and scientists with all research and development projects as assigned
- ❏ Inspected installations/systems to ensure that all applicable standards were consistently met
- ❏ Conducted ____ experiments with prototypes to test for ____
- ❏ Built prototypes and conducted product tests to meet all tolerance standards
- ❏ Completed product tests with ____% efficiency
- ❏ Gathered data, made calculations, and recorded test results accurately
- ❏ Conducted ____ statistical studies and analyzed ____ details
- ❏ Worked well with all assigned engineers and scientists
- ❏ Observed safety regulations and precautions at all times

Research and Development Engineer

- ❏ Investigated and evaluated all present systems now being used in the production process
- ❏ Researched and investigated new processes and equipment to meet new production goals
- ❏ Conducted feasibility studies to submit to management
- ❏ Completed all necessary engineering diagrams and layout drawings for test sites and equipment
- ❏ Created patent applications with drawings
- ❏ Improved production from ____ per ____ to ____ per ____ by implementing equipment modifications
- ❏ Developed new production methods that increased production and reduced waste
- ❏ Constructed sites for testing new designs and processes
- ❏ Designed and supervised the building of testing devices
- ❏ Collected and evaluated test data using a variety of statistical processes
- ❏ Prepared test results reports and bulletins to inform management of research results and recommendations
- ❏ Worked with manufacturing supervisors on improving efficiency of plant operations
- ❏ Supervised research technicians, assistants, and clerical workers with "good" to "excellent" ratings for supervision skills from subordinates
- ❏ Made routine recommendations for equipment purchases and new system modifications
- ❏ Created equipment budgets with ____% accuracy
- ❏ Kept up with industry state-of-the-art developments and new industry trends
- ❏ Demonstrated the ability to think outside the box to develop production solutions
- ❏ Possessed in-depth technical know-how and skills that enabled him to do an excellent job

Human Resources

Benefits Administrator

- ❏ Recommended and implemented benefit programs with ratings of ____ from ____% of employees
- ❏ Researched benefit plan changes and negotiated renewals with vendors to obtain the best benefit plan features
- ❏ Collected and compared experience and cost data to ensure organization employees got the best plan
- ❏ Handled employee questions and inquiries with ratings of ____ from ____% of employees
- ❏ Evaluated and revised internal procedures and processes to increase efficiency and reduce cost
- ❏ Interfaced with vendors and third-party administrators to resolve claim, policy, and coverage issues
- ❏ Filed accurate information in a timely manner and followed up with ____% accuracy
- ❏ Maintained compliance with government regulation changes
- ❏ Informed employees about the organization's 401(k) program and promoted participation
- ❏ Kept employees informed about the status of their claims and details of their plans
- ❏ Maintained employee benefit files and updated payroll records
- ❏ Developed and maintained online employee status change information
- ❏ Kept up on state of the industry and new trends
- ❏ Networked with industry experts and consultants
- ❏ Prepared data for actuarial assessments
- ❏ Reviewed short- and long-range cost estimates/projections and made recommendations for modifications
- ❏ Monitored administrative costs of benefit programs and recommended strategies for cost cutting

Compensation Analyst

- ❏ Researched pay scales for comparable jobs, including those of competitors, and developed competitive salary and benefit structures
- ❏ Evaluated proposed job remuneration packages and researched comparable jobs inside and outside the organization in order to establish salaries, hourly wages, and benefits packages
- ❏ Reviewed proposed wage increases and compensation packages to ensure parity
- ❏ Explained wage increase policies and considerations to supervisors
- ❏ Approved merit raises and other increases for employees with ____% satisfactory reviews by supervisors
- ❏ Reconciled pay rates and increases with budgets and alerted management of imbalances
- ❏ Retained ____% of employees due to salary and benefit increase recommendations
- ❏ Developed bonus, incentive, and recognition programs that received ____ positive ratings from supervisors
- ❏ Communicated organization's new programs to employees
- ❏ Maintained HR website for employee access to their job description and compensation information
- ❏ Prepared data for third-party wage and benefit surveys

Employee Relations Representative/ Labor Relations Representative

- ❏ Handled employee disputes with ____% "satisfactory" or better outcomes, as rated by the employees
- ❏ Worked successfully with managers to reduce employee turnover from ____% to ____%
- ❏ Created procedures for the organization's disciplinary actions
- ❏ Administered resignation and termination procedures with ____% "satisfactory" or better ratings from supervisors

- ❏ Maintained complete confidentiality on all employee dispute issues and employee complaints
- ❏ Reconciled employee grievances with skill and sensitivity
- ❏ Established a reputation as employees' advocate and gained the trust of employees
- ❏ Interceded between management and the union to promote cooperation
- ❏ Resolved ____ management/union conflicts with "satisfactory" or better outcomes, as rated by both sides
- ❏ Updated employee handbook
- ❏ Performed all pre-exit and post-exit employee interviews—for layoffs and terminations—with ____% "satisfactory" or better reviews by employees
- ❏ Represented the organization in employee legal issues with attorneys
- ❏ Investigated employee disputes and came up with solutions
- ❏ Counseled employees with advice consistent with organization policies and procedures

Recruiter

- ❏ Placed ads, posted opening notices (internally), and took steps to attract a large pool of qualified applicants
- ❏ Worked proactively to locate qualified candidates
- ❏ Monitored staffing proposals, turnovers, and hard-to-fill needs of all departments with "satisfactory" or better rating by managers
- ❏ Screened resumes and applications submitted for organization openings
- ❏ Selected the most qualified applicants and set up interviews
- ❏ Discussed position details with candidates
- ❏ Interviewed candidates and selected finalists
- ❏ Knew and followed all requirements for personal questions and inquiries of candidates

- ❏ Extended offers for employment to job finalists
- ❏ Maintained and tracked all employment records in compliance with EEO (Equal Employment Opportunity) requirements, and complied with all local, state, and federal employment regulations and laws
- ❏ Created and monitored succession planning for departments
- ❏ Represented the organization at job fairs and at on-campus recruitment sessions, keeping expenditures within the budget
- ❏ Administered tests for job skill assessment and suitability
- ❏ Investigated applications for work verification and recommendations, and eliminated unqualified candidates
- ❏ Reported pertinent findings of reference and background checks to supervisors
- ❏ Negotiated salary offers with candidate finalists and successfully hired the best
- ❏ Followed up with new hires during the probation/introduction period

Training Specialist

- ❏ Assessed needs for training programs
- ❏ Developed online courses for support personnel and managers
- ❏ Created, conducted, and monitored training courses in conjunction with organization managers
- ❏ Collected and analyzed employee production numbers to assess training needs
- ❏ Selected trainers, instructors, and coaches from employees and outside sources to teach needed skills
- ❏ Redesigned and improved training classes to increase training potential and reflect industry changes
- ❏ Checked trainees for skill and instruction retention ____ weeks after their programs with "good" to "excellent" results
- ❏ Surveyed managers to assess their needs for additional training programs

- Kept current on state of the industry in new techniques and learning methods
- Evaluated the impact of training, instruction, and coaching programs by measuring results in the workplace

Information Technology (IT)

Database Administrator
- Developed and managed database technologies for the organization
- Installed upgrades, fixed technical glitches, and monitored database performance
- Completed troubleshooting for ____ system procedures
- Provided technical support to ____ departments
- Devised, enforced, and maintained security measures and confidentiality policies so system remained secure
- Created a safe backup system for organization data and programs
- Developed programming guides and trained employees to use new database management procedures
- Used working knowledge of scripting languages
- Exhibited strong written and oral presentation skills
- Was able to prioritize ____ projects simultaneously
- Conducted quality test operations of new systems before organization-wide adoption

Data Entry Specialist/Data Entry Operator
- Input data with a proficiency rate of ___% accuracy
- Checked source data for errors and resolved any issues of possible errors
- Proofread input information for accuracy
- Updated data as it changed

- ❑ Possessed working knowledge of spreadsheet programs
- ❑ Completed general office tasks and duties maintaining an orderly work area
- ❑ Collected, maintained, and returned source documents to the proper department
- ❑ Checked with departments for approval of spreadsheet entries

Software Architect

- ❑ Spearheaded all the software development activities of the organization
- ❑ Managed the full software development life cycle (SDLC) for the organization
- ❑ Interfaced between organization managers and software designers (engineers/programmers) to communicate system software design needs
- ❑ Analyzed organization's present and future software and hardware needs
- ❑ Designed organization computer system, selected platforms, coding, and technical levels that best met present and future needs
- ❑ Reviewed all codes and supervised all software product testing
- ❑ Supervised software development team
- ❑ Won awards in industry competitions for design excellence
- ❑ Administered training sessions for users for each phase of the development cycle
- ❑ Tracked and maintained all records and metrics
- ❑ Ensured that all development practices remained in compliance with organization's best practices and procedures requirements
- ❑ Received "good" or better ratings from senior management for his overall performance

Software Engineer/Programmer

- ❑ Took management information and developed new applications to accommodate needs
- ❑ Created _____ new operating systems with _____% accuracy
- ❑ Tested _____ business applications and modified to an accuracy rate of _____%
- ❑ Adapted new business applications to existing systems with no disruption to work processes
- ❑ Developed business applications for new products

Systems Engineer/Systems Analyst

- ❑ Researched organization needs to determine computer system's present and future requirements
- ❑ Projected needs for all phases of the project life cycle
- ❑ Designed and implemented computer systems, software, and networks using managers' parameters
- ❑ Ensured software and hardware compatibility
- ❑ Determined system was capable of meeting performance metrics
- ❑ Recommended hardware changes, when necessary
- ❑ Created schedules of implementation and delivered on time
- ❑ Made budget projections and kept costs to within _____% of projections
- ❑ Set up trial systems to test for functional designs and capacity
- ❑ Completed troubleshooting for system glitches and errors

Legal

Attorney (for organization)

- ❑ Represented the organization and employees, advising them of their legal rights and obligations
- ❑ Reviewed business proposals, plans, and procedures for potential legal issues and problems

- ❏ Wrote modifications and changes to contracts to the advantage of the organization
- ❏ Provided legal counsel to the organization on compliance with government regulations
- ❏ Represented the organization and its employees in court
- ❏ Maintained positive relationships with a network of outside legal sources
- ❏ Reviewed corporate contracts and insurance claims against the organization and advised management on the proper procedures and actions to take in each case
- ❏ Wrote ____ business contracts (business to business and employee) that produced ____% successful outcomes
- ❏ Managed employee relations issues and handled union relationship conflicts with ____% success rate

Legal Assistant/Paralegal

- ❏ Kept corporate documents up to date, including all legal filings
- ❏ Prepared agendas and supporting documents for regular board legal staff meetings
- ❏ Provided support for annual stockholders meetings
- ❏ Prepared and secured approval of all board meeting minutes
- ❏ Scheduled depositions and prepared document indexes
- ❏ Possessed knowledge of legal litigation steps, processes, and required documents
- ❏ Helped draft all legal documents
- ❏ Filed proofs of claims and pleadings
- ❏ Made sure all organization legal fees were paid on time
- ❏ Supported attorney(s) in merger and acquisition details
- ❏ Assisted with the organization's internal legal transactions
- ❏ Drafted correspondence for attorney(s) on organization's ethics and compliance program

Manufacturing

Assembly Line Technician/Production Line Worker

- ❑ Interpreted schematics, drawings, blueprints, and written instructions accurately
- ❑ Assembled his assignment to within a ____% to ____% accuracy rate, and within the ____ per ____ time requirement
- ❑ Completed assignments with an error/waste factor of less than ____%
- ❑ Was capable of serving in ____ production tasks
- ❑ Was compliant with all safety regulations and precautions
- ❑ Informed supervisor of any production materials problems or safety issues
- ❑ Performed other duties as directed by supervisor
- ❑ Maintained tools in·high-performance working condition or notified supervisor of need for repairs
- ❑ Monitored material levels to keep assembly line operating at top performance rate
- ❑ Spotted imperfections and assembly errors ____% of the time

Machine Technician/Equipment Repairman

- ❑ Maintained and repaired machinery
- ❑ Monitored operation of ____ machines and cleaned ____ each ____
- ❑ Provided instructions to coworkers and assembly line personnel on proper routine maintenance procedures
- ❑ Kept maintenance records on ____ machines up to date
- ❑ Tested routinely for proper operation of ____ machines to ensure they were operating within specifications and tolerances
- ❑ Diagnosed operating problems with machinery and repaired them to function to specifications
- ❑ Performed setups of new machinery and completed preproduction testing
- ❑ Designed machines to meet production specifications

- ❏ Identified and recommended pieces of machinery to meet specific production functions
- ❏ Carried out preventive maintenance and calibration functions on ____ machines
- ❏ Maintained machinery consistent with safety regulations and safe operating condition and wore appropriate safety gear
- ❏ Checked operating procedures on machines to ensure that operating safety guidelines were being implemented
- ❏ Computed data and supplies and other relevant information on machinery as requested

Machinist

- ❏ Designed and built machine parts that operated to within ____% to ____% accuracy
- ❏ Used advanced knowledge of specialized equipment (calipers, drills, gauges, grinders, lathes, screw machines, etc.) to skillfully repair existing equipment
- ❏ Read blueprints, identified specifications and tolerances, and completed equipment setups
- ❏ Operated computerized equipment to build complex molds and dies
- ❏ Ran tests on replacement parts created to find whether they perform to within ____% to ____% of specifications

Plant Manager

- ❏ Understood his responsibility for ensuring the productive and safe operation of the plant
- ❏ Oversaw the daily production operations and kept production running to within ____% to ____% efficiency
- ❏ Checked on safety procedures each ___ and conducted safety drills each ____
- ❏ Set production goals of ____ per ____ and met them ____% of the time

- ❑ Received "good" or better ratings from subordinates for supervisory skills
- ❑ Kept subordinates motivated
- ❑ Trained subordinates for supervisory roles
- ❑ Monitored materials coming into and production going out of the plant and kept waste and loss to less than ____%

Production Supervisor

- ❑ Supervised production processes to keep operations proceeding at ____ units per ____ rate
- ❑ Worked to keep costs to within a ____ per ____ rate for his area of supervision
- ❑ Reduced waste during the review period from ____% to ____%
- ❑ Developed a cost-effective process that reduced cost by ____ per ____
- ❑ Received "good" or better ratings from subordinates for his supervisory skills
- ❑ Reduced overtime costs by ____% by carefully controlling parts and material supplies
- ❑ Interfaced with other departments to keep production flow at a high level
- ❑ Enforced all pertinent safety regulations and precautions

Scheduler

- ❑ Created a master schedule to ensure that all areas of the supply chain operated efficiently and on time
- ❑ Negotiated successfully for the delivery of supplies from ____ external vendors
- ❑ Expedited special deliveries when emergencies occurred
- ❑ Kept suppliers' deliveries on time ____% of the time
- ❑ Coordinated supply deliveries, production schedules, and shipping schedules with a ____% success rate

- Located and negotiated with multiple supply sources to maintain pricing and delivery requirements
- Interfaced with ____ customers during the course of the manufacturing process to ensure that the level of customer service met their expectations and requirements
- Monitored supply levels, orders, and due dates constantly to keep the organization's production and delivery commitments with a ____% on-time record
- Conducted production managers' meetings to maintain efficient schedule

Marketing, Advertising, Public Relations, and Social Media

Advertising Account Executive

- Served effectively as contact and link between organization/client, creative team, and media with a ____% success rate
- Scouted, researched, and developed prospects of ____ new companies or organizations/clients
- Conducted ____ discovery interviews with potential clients to assess their advertising needs
- Wrote ____ proposals for potential clients/organizations
- Made ____ presentations (pitches) to potential clients/organizations, which included complete ad campaigns, sample ads, media budgets, costs, and time-line estimates
- Monitored $_____ in budgeted accounts for clients/organization
- Sold ____ clients/organizations on the proposals he made for an estimated total of $_____ in new contracts for the review period
- Carried an advertising total of $_____ in annual client/organization account(s)
- Produced and revised media schedules and sales reports for ____ clients

- Directed and oversaw the creation of _____ new ads
- Managed _____ ongoing campaigns during the review period
- Worked with and directed a creative team of _____ to write copy, produce ads, and carry out campaign elements
- Bought television spots and time, newspaper space, billboard space, and online ad spots and time for _____ products
- Met client expectations and re-signed _____ clients to new contracts

Art Director/Creative Director

- Had a unique combination of creative and leadership skills that enabled him to visualize how messages could best be graphically expressed
- Worked cohesively and collaboratively with all advertising, marketing, and public relations personnel to ensure that the vision was realized
- Saw the big picture of how the products/services could best be promoted across mediums and markets to the best marketing advantage
- Integrated, strategically and effectively, all promotional pieces into a cohesive whole: television, newspaper, website, print materials, direct-mail pieces, social media, and promotional products
- Did not lose focus on the client's/organization's message, which resulted in _____% top-of-the-mind public awareness in marketing surveys
- Kept the brand image firmly in mind and foremost in all campaigns and advertising
- Oversaw _____ campaigns that came in _____% under budget
- Designed _____ websites that received high praise from clients/ organization management
- Laid out _____ websites that won awards for creativity
- Created _____ point-of-purchase retail displays for _____ clients/ organization products that raised sales _____%
- Developed and produced _____ detailed storyboards to illustrate how campaign elements and television ads would appear

- Created and oversaw ____ campaigns during the review period
- Participated in ____ client/organization presentations for new campaigns/products
- Represented the organization at ____ community, civic, and business conference events
- Hired and oversaw freelance copywriters, photographers, artists, craftsmen, and technicians to produce elements for campaigns
- Exhibited skillful use of a wide variety of computer software programs and used them with ____% proficiency

Brand Manager/Product Manager

- Headed up a team with personnel from market research, advertising, public relations, and sales to build brand/product equity
- Used creative marketing techniques to increase brand/product popularity among target consumers by ____%
- Created ____ programs to differentiate brand/product from those of competition
- Conducted ____ surveys and focus groups to analyze customer/consumer base and determine the demand for the product(s)
- Projected costs of all phases of marketing and sales efforts with ____% accuracy
- Set accurate budgets for marketing as ____% of projected brand/product sales
- Worked with advertising staff to develop brand/product trade show booth and materials and special promotional materials
- Analyzed effectiveness of promotional efforts with ____% accuracy
- Formed liaisons with marketing and advertising personnel to boost brand/product image among target market
- Analyzed sales results of brand/product(s) to determine direction for future product development
- Conducted ____ presentations to sales and marketing staff to keep their focus and pitches on new brand/product visions

- ❏ Supervised _____ assistant brand/product managers and _____ other personnel to ensure strategies were being executed properly
- ❏ Scheduled and timed product/brand releases to capitalize on unique market opportunities
- ❏ Kept up on state-of-the-art technologies for conveying brand/product awareness
- ❏ Researched and scouted competitive products/brands and other approaches for winning bigger market shares

Conference Coordinator/Event Planner

- ❏ Organized _____ events for _____ participants during the review period
- ❏ Focused on the event goals and planned effective meeting venues and areas around the theme
- ❏ Worked under extreme pressure due to location and catering glitches and still maintained an organized and successful event
- ❏ Maintained his cool in the face of subcontractor and hotel failures to produce as contracted
- ❏ Handled all details of the events with great efficiency
- ❏ Made extra efforts to understand the organization's goal, purpose, and message for the event in order to organize and carry it off effectively
- ❏ Did not drop a detail and created _____ events during the review period that resulted in "excellent" reviews by attendees
- ❏ Orchestrated event promotion, invitations, and follow-ups with _____ potential attendees
- ❏ Secured hotel and meeting room contracts, negotiating an average _____% discount
- ❏ Set a budget with management for the event and came in _____% under budget
- ❏ Arranged all special catering, luncheons, dinners, and cocktail hours
- ❏ Negotiated for and arranged attendees' Internet access, audiovisual equipment, and special-seating room arrangements

Copywriter

- ❏ Wrote persuasive copy on new product(s)/projects as directed
- ❏ Provided the copy for a wide variety of products and projects that received ____% approval from management reviewers
- ❏ Developed and wrote copy for product brochure copy, fact sheets, promotional emails, postcards, web pages, and/or social media
- ❏ Coordinated and worked well with advertising, marketing, and sales personnel to brainstorm themes and ideas for copy
- ❏ Met all deadlines for copy submission
- ❏ Monitored cultural trends and terms to make sure his messages were relevant and appropriate
- ❏ Used all relevant computer software programs to fit with organization's systems
- ❏ Was able to think creatively and in visual terms to come up with copy that worked for ____ products

Fundraising Manager

- ❏ Spearheaded efforts to implement a fundraising strategy
- ❏ Set target of $_____ as a goal for funds to be raised for the year
- ❏ Developed fundraising efforts of direct mail campaigns, wrote grant proposals to secure funds, cultivated major donor relationships, and secured endowments for a total of $_____ committed/pledged
- ❏ Budgeted for each fundraising effort and submitted budgets to management for approval
- ❏ Researched and expanded potential donor list from ____ to ____
- ❏ Made ____ potential donor contacts during the review period

Graphic Designer

- ❏ Brainstormed with advertising team to come up with ____ visual solutions and designs for ad, public relations, and marketing ideas
- ❏ Created thumbnail (concept) sketches and visual plans to help develop ideas
- ❏ Completed layouts and designs for direct mail pieces, publications, ads, and web pages
- ❏ Was responsible for selecting colors, artwork, and photography for approval of management
- ❏ Created charts and graphs as requested
- ❏ Used a wide variety of computer software programs proficiently to produce final work, including animated graphics
- ❏ Performed work that won "good" to "excellent" reviews from ____% of management

Marketing Account Executive

- ❏ Served effectively as link between the organization and customers/clients
- ❏ Had unique ability to build relationships with customers/clients by putting their needs first and foremost
- ❏ Identified ____ new market areas of potential customers/clients during the review period
- ❏ Analyzed ____ sets of research data to prioritize market segments for the organization
- ❏ Created ____ comparative studies with competitors to position organization products in a better competitive position
- ❏ Mastered productivity software and used it to track organization and competitors' sales of ____ products
- ❏ Wrote market reports that received "excellent" reviews from ____% of top-level management
- ❏ Created and initiated ____ product partners for ____ organization products
- ❏ Developed ____ new accounts for organization products

- ❑ Made ____ marketing strategy recommendations to top management, ____ of which were approved
- ❑ Participated in and coordinated with ____ advertising and creative staff on campaigns

Marketing Director/Marketing Manager/Strategic Marketing Manager/Social Media Marketing Specialist/Digital Strategist

- ❑ Created and implemented ____ new programs to get the word out about the brand/product/organization and increase awareness and interest
- ❑ Handled ____ promotions for the organization
- ❑ Oversaw ____ projects of creating a new logo, motto, product, and profitability assessment
- ❑ Used ____ platforms skillfully to market brand/product/organization, including print, broadcast media, Internet, direct mail, and social media
- ❑ Oversaw ____ organization website, social media, and email marketing campaigns
- ❑ Had in-depth knowledge of competitive products and their marketing techniques
- ❑ Kept an eye on current industry trends and the future of effective marketing
- ❑ Used excellent communication skills—written and verbal—as rated by ____% of top managers
- ❑ Implemented imaginative and innovative marketing concepts using a wide variety of computer-generated graphic designs that created ____ effective marketing vehicles
- ❑ Was ranked a top industry leader by ____% of top management

Market Research Analyst

❏ Researched and scouted competitors' markets and customers in order to develop savvy business and marketing plans

❏ Gathered secondary research information from reputable sources like Nielsen, Gallup, Forrester, Gale, and so on, in order to study key competitors and the demographics of their customers

❏ Analyzed macroeconomic conditions that impact sales in order to inform management of market forces

❏ Set up criteria and study to measure customer service, product satisfaction, and consumer termination

❏ Did ____ conjoint analysis to determine product awareness, trial, and usage tracking

❏ Analyzed data from ____ studies

❏ Wrote reports that highlighted the study results

❏ Designed ____ questionnaires, ____ marketing qualitative studies, and ____ focus group programs

❏ Contracted with moderators and marketing research agencies to conduct ____ special marketing projects

❏ Designed and implemented ____ social media campaigns that delivered valuable marketing information

❏ Managed marketing projects, including scheduling field work, and kept management informed on status and completion dates

❏ Helped management decide which products to sell, where to set product price points, and how and where best to sell them with a success rate of ____%

Media Planner/Media Buyer/Communications Planner/ Brand Strategist/Social Media Strategist

❏ Worked as an effective member of the advertising and public relations teams

❏ Possessed current knowledge of all effective media outlets—print, television, radio, outdoor, social media, and interview—and their efficacy for the organization's needs

- ❏ Did an excellent job of creating effective media mixes to promote/advertise products
- ❏ Maintained good relationships with media representatives
- ❏ Purchased media within the budget and resolved all media problems
- ❏ Demonstrated effective postcampaign analysis skills

Public Relations Account Executive

- ❏ Created ____ unique plans for building positive public images of the organization/client in the minds of the general public
- ❏ Developed and placed ____ stories about the organization/client making positive contributions in ____ newspapers, ____ online blogs, social media, and on ____ local television programs
- ❏ Wrote ____ press releases on organization/client programs and personnel that he placed in ____ media outlets
- ❏ Set up ____ interviews for magazine writers, online bloggers, journalists, and editors with organization/client personnel to present new developments and products
- ❏ Arranged interviews for ____ feature story/stories in ____ magazines that focused on the organization/client and personnel
- ❏ Networked with community leaders to obtain speaking engagements for ____ organization/client managers/representatives
- ❏ Arranged for organization/client sponsorship of ____ community programs, which raised organization awareness by ____%
- ❏ Wrote ____ speeches for organization/client managers, which audience members rated "good" or better
- ❏ Developed organization/client plant visitor programs for college career days programs
- ❏ Created organization/client logos and ____ visuals to be used at trade shows
- ❏ Developed social media campaigns for organization's/client's representatives to interact with customers
- ❏ Initiated the organization's/client's participation in ____ local programs, including employees' fitness; "green" living; and resources, recycling, and conservation

Publicist

- ❑ Garnered ____ positive mentions for the organization in newspapers, magazines, online blogs, and social media
- ❑ Built and maintained effective relationships with local, regional, and national print media and screen journalists who could help shed positive light on the organization
- ❑ Maintained up-to-date media and online contact indexes
- ❑ Developed ____ outstanding pieces for press kits
- ❑ Prepared fact sheets, Q&As, press releases, biographies, public service announcements, brochures, newsletters, and social media campaigns
- ❑ Pitched ____ story and feature ideas to local business publications and online sources
- ❑ Wrote ____ press releases on organization personnel, programs, and products that were published in ____ media outlets and on ____ online outlets
- ❑ Screened ____ print and screen journalists by researching and reading their published stories
- ❑ Created online buzz for the organization through creative networking with bloggers and posting on fan websites and social media pages
- ❑ Demonstrated excellent written and verbal communication skills
- ❑ Remained calm during times of extreme stress and met critical deadlines ____% of the time
- ❑ Represented the organization very well in community meetings and programs
- ❑ Prepared ____ presentations to make to potential donor groups and prospects
- ❑ Maintained and updated donor databases, working with fundraising committees
- ❑ Oversaw event planning and coordinated with event planners as needed

Operations and Distribution

Administrative Assistant

- ❑ Kept tabs on ____ transactional duties to keep his supervisor's office running smoothly
- ❑ Was rated ____ by coworkers and managers in his ability to coordinate information and set up meetings
- ❑ Received visitor ratings of ____ to ____ for making a positive impression of the organization and being helpful in serving as his supervisor's first point of contact
- ❑ Exhibited excellent skills in drafting correspondence and other communications for his supervisor
- ❑ Displayed excellent oral presentation skills when called upon
- ❑ Handled all telephone calls tactfully
- ❑ Kept supervisor's calendar and made changes and follow-up contacts
- ❑ Was responsible for archiving institutional history of the organization and organizing and maintaining files

Clerk/Clerical Staff Employee

- ❑ Provided general support services and performed a variety of office duties as directed
- ❑ Managed electronic and paper files with ____% accuracy
- ❑ Created spreadsheets, managed databases, and created reports and documents as directed
- ❑ Used presentation and design software to enhance reports and documents with ____% proficiency
- ❑ Communicated with clients and customers using email, the organization's website, and mail with ____% or better satisfaction rating
- ❑ Arranged meetings and conference calls
- ❑ Was able to multitask in performing computer input, faxing, telephone contacts, and copying with a ____% or better satisfactory rating

- ❏ Completed data entry work on the computer, including spreadsheets with a speed of ____ per ____ and an accuracy rate of ____%
- ❏ Proofed and checked data input accuracy with a ____% or better satisfaction rating
- ❏ Handled customer complaints resulting from clerical errors with a ____% or better satisfaction rating
- ❏ Interfaced with vendors to order supplies
- ❏ Made travel arrangements, with a ____% success rating
- ❏ Kept inventories of needed supplies at a ____% or better satisfactory rating
- ❏ Prepared invoices and receipts with ____% accuracy
- ❏ Supervised ____ clerical personnel with a ____% or better satisfactory rating
- ❏ Hired and trained ____ clerical staff members, maintaining a turnover rate of less than ____%

Customer Service Representative/Customer Service Associate

- ❏ Answered inquires with authority and to a customers' satisfaction rating of ____%
- ❏ Created new customers by going the extra mile, diagnosing and creating solutions to their problems
- ❏ Displayed complete knowledge of the organization's products and services
- ❏ Understood the organization's policies and procedures completely and applied them properly to get customers' problems solved
- ❏ Was rated "good" or better by customers in handling their problems quickly and completely
- ❏ Was creative in solving current customers' problems
- ❏ Improved his rating from ____% customer satisfaction to ____% by getting feedback and making changes
- ❏ Delivered what and when he promised to customers
- ❏ Resolved billing problems to customers' satisfaction ____% of the time
- ❏ Up-sold products to customers ____% of the time

- Referred extraordinary problems to the proper manager ____% of the time
- Used all modes of contact expertly: telephone, email, fax, mail, and special delivery
- Processed renewals, returns, exchanges, and service calls to within a ____% to ____% efficiency rating
- Created trust with customers that reflected well on the organization
- Displayed excellent writing skills
- Dealt with difficult customers very well, and resolved ____% of the situations satisfactorily
- Used computer applications and did basic math well

Maintenance Supervisor/Operations and Maintenance Manager

- Supervised ____ of the organization's maintenance employees, ____ outside tradesmen, and ____ contract workers to keep the physical plant safe, clean, and operating at maximum efficiency
- Was responsible for keeping computerized inventory and stock management programs up to date and capable of meeting organization's needs
- Maintained lists of subcontractors and contractors who could supply needed services and products
- Estimated costs for new projects of construction and physical plant changes
- Specified new design and construction projects
- Worked with ____ outside architectural and building engineering firms to develop plans and designs
- Negotiated with ____ contractors and subcontractors to obtain the best and most cost-effective services and supplies
- Allocated space for departmental expansion and was responsible for the purchase of equipment
- Was responsible for transport services and recycling
- Oversaw renovation(s) and brought the project(s) in at ____% under budget

- ❑ Monitored utility usage and developed ____ plans for energy savings of ____ %

- ❑ Completed long-term plans for maintenance and modernization of ____ buildings

- ❑ Kept physical facilities in compliance with local and national governmental codes and regulations

- ❑ Was proactive in ensuring adherence to all safety regulations and precautions and maintained a record of zero on-the-job accidents

- ❑ Inspected construction projects and installations

- ❑ Oversaw exterior maintenance, landscaping, and snow removal

Office Manager

- ❑ Set a fine example for office personnel by being at work early and starting to work on time ____% of the time

- ❑ Oversaw office personnel, making sure business was running in a smooth and efficient manner ____% of the time

- ❑ Motivated office personnel to increase work volume and accuracy by ____% by using incentive programs

- ❑ Maintained supplies for office staff and ordered additional supplies as needed

- ❑ Monitored office budget and kept expenditures to within ____% below budget

- ❑ Forecast office equipment needs and created budgets with ____% success

- ❑ Selected office equipment for purchase and rental

- ❑ Handled all equipment maintenance and repairs with outside service contractors

- ❑ Completed billing and payroll with an error rate of less than ____%

- ❑ Hired and trained new employees for the office functions

- ❑ Conducted new office employee orientation and administered training

- ❑ Administered discipline of office employees with positive outcomes ____% of the time

Receptionist

- ❏ Presented a cheerful and welcoming face of the organization to visitors
- ❏ Maintained a professional relationship with visitors and clients
- ❏ Handled basic communications with visitors, clients, and staff members with a ____% satisfaction rating
- ❏ Extended visitor courtesies and answered questions and requests with professionalism with a ____% satisfaction or better rating
- ❏ Carried out an array of duties involved in processing visitors and clients coming into the organization, including checking in, creating visitor badges, giving directions, and ushering the visitors to various offices
- ❏ Notified employees of arriving visitors in a timely and efficient manner
- ❏ Followed organizational procedures for dealing with visitor area problems and conflicts
- ❏ Completed mail processing and special small deliveries with a ____% satisfaction or better rating
- ❏ Carried out the organization's visitor restrictions and other policies successfully
- ❏ Maintained reception area schedule and services, earning a ____% satisfaction or better rating
- ❏ Helped with general office work overload duties as directed by the office manager with a ____% satisfaction or better rating

Security Manager/Head of Security

- ❏ Oversaw security operations for the organization
- ❏ Developed and enforced security policies for management's approval with a ____% satisfaction or better rating
- ❏ Identified ____ possible areas for security breaches and implemented changes to eliminate them
- ❏ Conducted routine criminal background checks and physical and drug screening for security candidates

- Supervised security team of ____ with subordinates' rating of "good" or better
- Ensured the organization's security practices met local, state, and federal guidelines with regard to emergencies and security, including OSHA requirements
- Developed evacuation and emergency procedures for employees, and conducted departmental evacuation drills
- Worked with local officials to develop a disaster plan for the organization
- Conducted safety drills for employees during the review period
- Reviewed employee injury and accident reports, investigated, and instituted procedural changes to eliminate hazards with a ____% success rate
- Inspected and tested security alarm system, fire suppression system, and all area fire extinguishers every ____
- Recommended new safety procedures and equipment replacements
- Maintained up-to-date inspection and maintenance records for all safety and disaster equipment
- Maintained control of all security system codes and secure-area admission badges
- Interfaced with insurance company, accompanied inspectors on facility inspections, and made changes to meet requirements
- Served as liaison with local law enforcement and assisted in ____ investigations of accidents, thefts, and property loss incidents
- Hired, trained, and coordinated security personnel work schedules to ensure a safe and secure work environment at all times with ____% satisfaction or better rating

Stock Clerk

- Received merchandise, counted it, and inspected it for damage and defects with ____% accuracy
- Reported damage and defects of incoming products to supervisor

- Marked new products with identification tags and price labels with ____% accuracy and acceptable or better speed and proficiency
- Stocked new products on the sales floors
- Maintained sales floor aisles and walkways, keeping them free of clutter and product packaging, and safe for customers
- Reshelved and straightened sales floor areas to maintain a safe and customer-pleasant environment
- Performed special stocking and restocking tasks as directed by supervisor with "good" proficiency and accuracy

Transportation Supervisor/Traffic Services Manager

- Kept all transport records, including time sheets, inventory records, and work orders, on the computerized system with ____% accuracy
- Scheduled the delivery of products with an on-time record of ____% to ____%
- Maintained up-to-date service records on all transportation equipment
- Performed routine maintenance and service on all transportation equipment
- Set schedules, established efficient routes and deliveries, arranged dispatches, and solved logistical issues for drivers
- Created tracking data on computerized system for customers to use with ____% accuracy rating
- Communicated with customers on conflicts, complaints, and delays with customer-rated level of "satisfaction" or better
- Coordinated with outside organizations to create return-trip cargo loads, producing profits of $_____
- Created ____ cost-control program(s) that reduced shipping costs by ____%
- Met on-time delivery schedules ____% of the time
- Received ____ complaints for shipping-damaged goods
- Hired and trained ____ employees with ____% turnover rate
- Was responsible for assessing the tools, equipment, and manpower necessary for transportation needs

Sales

Cashier/Checker

- ❏ Operated the cash register proficiently
- ❏ Handled cash, credit cards, and check payments consistent with company policy and procedures, verifying credit as necessary
- ❏ Balanced cash register receipts and cash drawer balance according to company policy with ____% proficiency
- ❏ Greeted customers in a welcoming and cordial manner and conversed with each, consistent with company-prescribed follow-up comments
- ❏ Answered customer questions about products and contacted the proper personnel to resolve pricing, merchandise problems, and return issues according to company policy
- ❏ Processed all special sales, coupons, and gift cards according to company policy
- ❏ Ensured that all computerized prices accurately reflected featured specials
- ❏ Contacted management and security in cases of any safety or theft issues
- ❏ Kept checkout area organized and clean
- ❏ Processed return merchandise as directed by company policy and procedures at ____% of "excellent"
- ❏ Performed other tasks as directed during slow periods
- ❏ Directed customers to the proper store area to purchase or exchange products

Sales Account Executive

- ❏ Developed database and initiated contact with ____ potential customers/clients
- ❏ Converted ____% of sales prospects into customers/clients in the review period
- ❏ Made ____ sales presentations with a conversion rate of ____%

- ❑ Was responsible for new sales of $_____ dollars in products to customers/clients
- ❑ Developed and screened ____ new prospects
- ❑ Researched and set sales targets for all ____ geographical areas under his direction for the next ____
- ❑ Created the "best sales steps" plan that resulted in a ____% sales conversion rate
- ❑ Conducted needs analyses for ____ client/customer groups
- ❑ Exceeded sales goals by ____% for all his accounts
- ❑ Outproduced all other sales account executives by ___%
- ❑ Retained ____% of existing customers/clients
- ❑ Resold existing customers/clients at the rate of ____% repeat sales
- ❑ Rated in the top ____% in potential customers record keeping
- ❑ Perfected sales strategies that increased closings by ____%

Sales Assistant (Retail)

- ❑ Demonstrated in-depth product knowledge
- ❑ Answered customer questions and inquiries at a ____% satisfactory or better rate
- ❑ Was able to skillfully perform product demonstrations
- ❑ Increased sales volume of promoted products by ____%
- ❑ Rated competent, professional, courteous, and cordial by ____% of customers
- ❑ Maintained an orderly and appealing demonstration area

Sales Associate (Retail)

- ❑ Exhibited customer service skills of "excellent" ____% of the time
- ❑ Communicated effectively with customers to understand unique needs and requests
- ❑ Built a repeat relationship with a customer base of ____
- ❑ Was requested by returning customers ____ times

- ❑ Met or surpassed his sales quotas ____% of the time
- ❑ Processed, tagged, inspected, and reshelved returns in his area
- ❑ Kept company security, theft, and damage prevention policies in his area
- ❑ Used company alterations and repair services skillfully to increase sales and customer satisfaction
- ❑ Rated at ____% by other sales associates in ability to work harmoniously to refer customers and meet their needs
- ❑ Demonstrated in-depth product knowledge and was able to explain product features and benefits to ____% customer satisfaction rate
- ❑ Was willing to go the distance to meet unique and unusual customer requests to locate products and solve problems ____% of the time
- ❑ Displayed products to make the customer shopping experience flow seamlessly through his area
- ❑ Demonstrated understanding of how consumers make brand and style selections
- ❑ Calculated discounts and promotions to a customer-satisfaction rate of ____% of "good" or better
- ❑ Made sure the correct amount of money and change for the shift was available in the cash register
- ❑ Reconciled the cash register at/after closing with a correct balance ____% of the time
- ❑ Handled returns and exchanges on all items according to company policy and procedures
- ❑ Tracked and counted inventory with a ____% accuracy rate

Sales Manager

- ❑ Acquired ____ new customers/clients through direct sales techniques
- ❑ Completed ____ cold calls and ____ business-to-business marketing visits, converting ____% to sales

- ❑ Was successful in developing ____ technical and sales management processes
- ❑ Oversaw the sales staff of ____ persons effectively, increasing sales by ____%
- ❑ Implemented ____ new marketing strategies, which resulted in an increase in sales by ____%
- ❑ Instituted ____ new procedures for project management
- ❑ Trained ____ new sales personnel, developing their sales skills and techniques to a proficient level
- ❑ Managed sales personnel with a rating of ____% "excellent" scores by subordinates
- ❑ Reduced sales staff turnover by ____%
- ❑ Motivated sales staff by instituting ____ bonus and incentive programs
- ❑ Monitored sales staff performance and helped sales personnel increase their customer satisfaction rates by ____%
- ❑ Oversaw sales personnel compliance with all applicable policies and procedures
- ❑ Projected sales volumes for review period with a ____% accuracy rate
- ❑ Gave feedback to manufacturers on customer satisfaction rates, complaints, and design suggestions
- ❑ Developed and assigned sales books and quotas to sales personnel
- ❑ Completed all sales reports and requirements with a ____% satisfactory or above rating
- ❑ Ensured that ____% of the sales team met or exceeded their sales quotas
- ❑ Hired and mentored ____ sales personnel during the review period
- ❑ Conducted ____ sales campaigns that resulted in a ____% sales increase

Sales Representative (Outbound/Outside)

❑ Demonstrated consistently persuasive telephone skills

❑ Turned ____% of leads into sales by carefully qualifying potential customers

❑ Used very skillful techniques to lead customers through the sales steps, addressing each concern and gaining their confidence

❑ Rated ____% effective in sales presentations

❑ Kept all manufacturers' restrictions on policies, procedures, territories, and so on carefully

❑ Worked with manufacturers to make recommendations for product changes, accessories, and packaging

❑ Farmed assigned territory and created ____ new customers

❑ Represented manufacturers and suppliers with a ____% "satisfaction" or above rating

❑ Ensured credit-worthy leads in all cases before initiating sales

❑ Used all avenues available to retain ____% customer satisfaction after the sale

❑ Met or exceeded sales quotas

❑ Gleaned valuable marketing and product modification information from customers, which he submitted to the proper personnel

❑ Helped manufacturers understand and interpret customer needs and criteria

❑ Outpaced competitors' sales by ____%

❑ Empathized with customers and gained their confidence and commitment

❑ Retained customers and had a ____% repeat sales percentage

❑ Maintained prospective/active leads lists of ____ by prequalifying and strategizing repeat contacts

Telemarketer/Call Center Agent/Telesales Representative

- ❏ Pitched _____ people over the telephone and presented products/services during the review period
- ❏ Completed _____ surveys over the telephone during the review period
- ❏ Was successful in securing $_____ in donations/sales
- ❏ Executed _____ sales for service contracts and renewals during the review period
- ❏ Enlivened script with an engaging conversational tone and by relating to potential buyers
- ❏ Sold _____ of every _____ calls made during the review period
- ❏ Possessed in-depth knowledge of the products/services and was able to convey that to potential buyers
- ❏ Overcame prospects' objections with sound presentation and distinction between features and benefits
- ❏ Answered all customers' questions and queries about services/products
- ❏ Presented features and benefits without overpromising
- ❏ Scheduled _____ sales presentation appointments with potential customers who wished to learn more about the product(s) during the review period

APPENDIX 1
Use Strong Action Verbs

Use strong, precise action verbs—present or past tense—to express an employee's performance. Try these:

A

- Accelerated
- Accentuated
- Accepted
- Acclimated
- Accommodated
- Accomplished
- Accounted (for)
- Achieved
- Acquainted
- Acquired
- Acted
- Activated
- Actuated

- Adapted
- Addressed
- Adhered
- Adjusted
- Administered
- Adopted
- Advanced
- Advised
- Advocated
- Affirmed
- Aided
- Aligned
- Allocated
- Allowed

- Amplified
- Analyzed
- Anticipated
- Apologized
- Applied
- Appointed
- Appraised
- Appreciated
- Approached
- Appropriated
- Approved
- Arranged
- Articulated
- Ascended

- Ascertained
- Aspired
- Assembled
- Asserted
- Assessed
- Assigned
- Assimilated
- Assisted
- Assumed
- Assured
- Attained
- Attempted
- Attended
- Audited
- Augmented
- Authorized
- Automated
- Averted
- Avoided

B

- Balanced
- Behaved
- Believed
- Broadened
- Budgeted
- Built

C

- Calculated
- Capitalized
- Capitulated

- Captivated
- Captured
- Catalogued
- Categorized
- Centralized
- Chaired
- Challenged
- Championed
- Charted
- Checked
- Circulated
- Clarified
- Classified
- Cleared
- Coached
- Coded
- Collaborated
- Collected
- Combined
- Commanded
- Commented
- Committed
- Communicated
- Compared
- Compelled
- Compensated
- Compiled
- Completed
- Complied
- Composed

- Comprehended
- Compressed
- Computed
- Conceived
- Concentrated
- Conceptualized
- Concluded
- Condensed
- Conducted
- Conferred
- Configured
- Confined
- Conformed
- Conjectured
- Connected
- Considered
- Consigned
- Consolidated
- Constructed
- Consulted
- Consummated
- Contemplated
- Continued
- Contributed
- Controlled
- Converted
- Conveyed
- Cooperated
- Coordinated
- Coped

- ❑ Corrected
- ❑ Counseled
- ❑ Created
- ❑ Critiqued
- ❑ Cultivated
- ❑ Customized

D

- ❑ Debated
- ❑ Debugged
- ❑ Decentralized
- ❑ Decreased
- ❑ Dedicated
- ❑ Defined
- ❑ Delayed
- ❑ Delegated
- ❑ Delivered
- ❑ Demonstrated
- ❑ Deployed
- ❑ Designated
- ❑ Designed
- ❑ Detected
- ❑ Determined
- ❑ Developed
- ❑ Deviated (from)
- ❑ Devised
- ❑ Devoted
- ❑ Diagnosed
- ❑ Directed
- ❑ Disciplined
- ❑ Discovered

- ❑ Discussed
- ❑ Dispersed
- ❑ Displayed
- ❑ Dissected
- ❑ Disseminated
- ❑ Distinguished
- ❑ Distributed
- ❑ Documented
- ❑ Drafted

E

- ❑ Earned
- ❑ Edified
- ❑ Edited
- ❑ Elevated
- ❑ Elicited
- ❑ Eliminated
- ❑ Emanated
- ❑ Embellished
- ❑ Embraced
- ❑ Emphasized
- ❑ Employed
- ❑ Empowered
- ❑ Emulated
- ❑ Enabled
- ❑ Encompassed
- ❑ Encouraged
- ❑ Energized
- ❑ Enforced
- ❑ Engaged
- ❑ Engendered

- ❑ Enhanced
- ❑ Enlarged
- ❑ Enlightened
- ❑ Enriched
- ❑ Ensured
- ❑ Established
- ❑ Estimated
- ❑ Evaluated
- ❑ Evoked
- ❑ Examined
- ❑ Exceeded
- ❑ Excelled
- ❑ Executed
- ❑ Exemplified
- ❑ Exercised
- ❑ Exerted
- ❑ Exhibited
- ❑ Expanded
- ❑ Expected
- ❑ Expedited
- ❑ Expended
- ❑ Experimented
- ❑ Exploited
- ❑ Explored
- ❑ Expressed
- ❑ Extended
- ❑ Extracted
- ❑ Extrapolated
- ❑ Exuded

F

- Faced
- Facilitated
- Factored (in)
- Figured
- Fixated (on)
- Fixed
- Flagged
- Focused
- Followed (up)
- Forecasted
- Foresaw
- Forestalled
- Forged
- Formed
- Formulated
- Fostered
- Found
- Fronted (for)
- Fulfilled
- Furnished
- Furthered

G

- Gained
- Gathered
- Gave
- Generated
- Gestured
- Guessed
- Guided

H

- Handled
- Heads
- Helped
- Highlighted
- Hosted

I

- Identified
- Illustrated
- Impacted
- Imparted
- Implemented
- Impressed
- Improved
- Improvised
- Increased
- Individualized
- Influenced
- Informed
- Initiated
- Innovated
- Insisted
- Inspected
- Installed
- Instigated
- Instilled
- Instituted
- Instructed
- Insured
- Integrated

- Interacted (with)
- Interfaced (with)
- Interpreted
- Intervened
- Interviewed
- Introduced
- Intuited
- Invented
- Investigated
- Invigorated
- Isolated
- Issued
- Itemized

J

- Judged
- Justified

K

- Kept
- Kindled
- Knew

L

- Launched
- Lead
- Learned
- Lectured
- Legislated
- Lent
- Let
- Leveraged
- Limited

- ❏ Listened
- ❏ Lobbied
- ❏ Logged

M

- ❏ Made
- ❏ Maintained
- ❏ Managed
- ❏ Manifested
- ❏ Manipulated
- ❏ Marketed
- ❏ Maximized
- ❏ Measured
- ❏ Mediated
- ❏ Merged
- ❏ Met
- ❏ Minimized
- ❏ Mobilized
- ❏ Modified
- ❏ Monitored
- ❏ Motivated

N

- ❏ Navigated
- ❏ Necessitated
- ❏ Needed
- ❏ Negated
- ❏ Negotiated
- ❏ Neutralized
- ❏ Notified
- ❏ Nurtured

O

- ❏ Observed
- ❏ Obtained
- ❏ Operated
- ❏ Optimized
- ❏ Orchestrated
- ❏ Ordered
- ❏ Organized
- ❏ Originated
- ❏ Overcame
- ❏ Overhauled
- ❏ Oversaw

P

- ❏ Paced
- ❏ Participated
- ❏ Perceived
- ❏ Performed
- ❏ Perpetuated
- ❏ Persuaded
- ❏ Planned
- ❏ Possessed
- ❏ Postponed
- ❏ Practiced
- ❏ Predicted
- ❏ Prepared
- ❏ Presented
- ❏ Presided
- ❏ Presumed
- ❏ Prevented
- ❏ Prioritized

- ❏ Processed
- ❏ Procured
- ❏ Produced
- ❏ Programmed
- ❏ Progressed
- ❏ Projected
- ❏ Promoted
- ❏ Proposed
- ❏ Protected
- ❏ Protested
- ❏ Provided
- ❏ Publicized
- ❏ Purchased
- ❏ Purged
- ❏ Pursued

Q

- ❏ Qualified
- ❏ Quantified
- ❏ Queried
- ❏ Questioned
- ❏ Quoted

R

- ❏ Radiated
- ❏ Radicalized
- ❏ Recognized
- ❏ Recommended
- ❏ Reconciled
- ❏ Recorded
- ❏ Recruited
- ❏ Redeemed

- ❏ Redirected
- ❏ Reduced
- ❏ Referred
- ❏ Refined
- ❏ Reflected
- ❏ Regarded
- ❏ Registered
- ❏ Regulated
- ❏ Reinforced
- ❏ Reinvented
- ❏ Rejected
- ❏ Rejuvenated
- ❏ Relied (on)
- ❏ Rendered
- ❏ Reorganized
- ❏ Repaired
- ❏ Replaced
- ❏ Reported
- ❏ Represented
- ❏ Required
- ❏ Researched
- ❏ Resolved
- ❏ Resonated
- ❏ Respected
- ❏ Restored
- ❏ Restructured
- ❏ Retained
- ❏ Reviewed
- ❏ Revised
- ❏ Revitalized

- ❏ Rewarded
- ❏ Risked
- ❏ Routed

S

- ❏ Satisfied
- ❏ Scheduled
- ❏ Secured
- ❏ Seized
- ❏ Selected
- ❏ Served
- ❏ Settled
- ❏ Shared
- ❏ Showed
- ❏ Simplified
- ❏ Simulated
- ❏ Sold
- ❏ Solicited
- ❏ Solved
- ❏ Sought
- ❏ Sourced
- ❏ Sparked
- ❏ Spearheaded
- ❏ Specialized
- ❏ Specified
- ❏ Strengthened
- ❏ Strived
- ❏ Structured
- ❏ Studied
- ❏ Submitted
- ❏ Substantiated

- ❏ Suggested
- ❏ Summarized
- ❏ Supervised
- ❏ Supplemented
- ❏ Supplied
- ❏ Supported
- ❏ Surmounted
- ❏ Surpassed
- ❏ Surveyed
- ❏ Sustained
- ❏ Synchronized
- ❏ Synthesized
- ❏ Systemized

T

- ❏ Tailored
- ❏ Targeted
- ❏ Taught
- ❏ Terminated
- ❏ Tested
- ❏ Thought
- ❏ Thrilled
- ❏ Thrived
- ❏ Told
- ❏ Tolerated
- ❏ Took
- ❏ Traced
- ❏ Tracked
- ❏ Trained
- ❏ Transacted
- ❏ Transformed

- ❑ Translated
- ❑ Transmitted
- ❑ Treated
- ❑ (Did) Troubleshooting

U

- ❑ Uncovered
- ❑ Underrated
- ❑ Underscored
- ❑ Understood
- ❑ Undertook
- ❑ Unified
- ❑ United
- ❑ Updated

- ❑ Upended
- ❑ Upgraded
- ❑ Uploaded
- ❑ Upset
- ❑ Upstaged
- ❑ Used
- ❑ Utilized

V

- ❑ Validated
- ❑ Varied
- ❑ Verified
- ❑ Viewed
- ❑ Visualized

- ❑ Vitalized
- ❑ Volunteered

W

- ❑ Wedged
- ❑ Weighed
- ❑ Welcomed
- ❑ Widened
- ❑ Winnowed
- ❑ Won
- ❑ Worked
- ❑ Wrote

Y

- ❑ Yielded

APPENDIX 2
Use Qualifying Adverbs

Adverbs, those colorful "ly" words, can be useful to describe the exact degree of something, or they can add an unnecessary and muddying opacity to something that was clearly stated. Don't use adverbs when you can use exact numbers and clear statements of fact. Do use them when they add definition to your evaluation. Here are some choices you may want to consider:

A
- ❏ Abundantly
- ❏ Absolutely
- ❏ Accurately
- ❏ Actively
- ❏ Adeptly
- ❏ Adequately
- ❏ Aggressively
- ❏ Always
- ❏ Alertly
- ❏ Ambitiously

- ❏ Appropriately
- ❏ Assertively
- ❏ Attentively

B
- ❏ Basically
- ❏ Belatedly

C
- ❏ Calmly
- ❏ Capably
- ❏ Carefully
- ❏ Cautiously

- ❏ Clearly
- ❏ Closely
- ❏ Cohesively
- ❏ Collaboratively
- ❏ Compellingly
- ❏ Competently
- ❏ Completely
- ❏ Comprehensively
- ❏ Concisely
- ❏ Confidently
- ❏ Conscientiously

- Considerably
- Consistently
- Constructively
- Continually
- Continuously
- Cooperatively
- Correctly
- Courageously
- Courteously
- Creatively

D

- Decisively
- Definitely
- Deliberately
- Dependably
- Deservedly
- Determinedly
- Diligently
- Diplomatically
- Discreetly
- Distinctively
- Dynamically

E

- Eagerly
- Effectively
- Efficiently
- Eminently
- Energetically
- Enthusiastically
- Exactly

- Exceptionally
- Excessively
- Extraordinarily
- Extremely

F

- Factually
- Fairly
- Favorably
- Flawlessly
- Flexibly
- Formidably
- Frankly
- Frequently

G

- Generously
- Genuinely
- Good-naturedly
- Gracefully
- Greatly

H

- Harmoniously
- Helpfully
- Highly
- Honestly

I

- Imaginatively
- Immediately
- Immensely
- Impeccably
- Importantly

- Independently
- Industriously
- Influentially
- Ingeniously
- Innovatively
- Instantly
- Instinctively
- Instrumentally
- Intensely
- Intentionally
- Intently
- Interactively
- Interestingly
- Intermittently
- Inventively

J

- Judiciously
- Justifiably
- Justly

K

- Keenly
- Kindly
- Knowingly

L

- Lastingly
- Latently
- Lively
- Logically
- Loyally

M

- Magnificently
- Majorly
- Masterfully
- Maturely
- Meaningfully
- Methodically
- Meticulously

N

- Naturally
- Neatly
- Necessarily
- Normally

O

- Objectively
- Observantly
- Obviously
- Openly
- Open-mindedly
- Opportunistically
- Optimally
- Optimistically
- Orderly
- Originally
- Outstandingly
- Overly

P

- Partially
- Patiently
- Perfectly

- Periodically
- Persistently
- Persuasively
- Pleasantly
- Politely
- Positively
- Powerfully
- Pragmatically
- Precisely
- Predictably
- Predominantly
- Proactively
- Productively
- Professionally
- Proficiently
- Profoundly
- Profusely
- Progressively
- Prolifically
- Prominently
- Properly
- Punctually
- Purposefully
- Purposely

Q

- Questioningly
- Quickly

R

- Rapidly
- Rationally

- Readily
- Realistically
- Reassuringly
- Regularly
- Relentlessly
- Reliably
- Remarkably
- Repeatedly
- Resourcefully
- Respectfully
- Responsibly
- Responsively
- Rigorously
- Routinely

S

- Safely
- Satisfactorily
- Seemingly
- Self-confidently
- Self-demandingly
- Sequentially
- Seriously
- Sharply
- Significantly
- Sincerely
- Sizably
- Soundly
- Splendidly
- Steadfastly
- Steadily

- Sternly
- Strategically
- Strictly
- Stridently
- Strongly
- Subjectively
- Substantially
- Successfully
- Succinctly
- Suddenly
- Superbly
- Supportively
- Surprisingly
- Sustainably
- Swiftly
- Sympathetically
- Synergistically
- Systematically

T
- Tactfully
- Tactically
- Tediously
- Thankfully
- Thoroughly
- Thoughtfully
- Timely
- Truthfully
- Typically

U
- Ultimately
- Unexpectedly
- Uniformly
- Unintentionally
- Uniquely
- Unnecessarily
- Unusually

- Urgently
- Usefully
- Usually

V
- Validly
- Valuably
- Viably
- Vibrantly
- Vigorously
- Voluntarily

W
- Willfully
- Willingly
- Winningly
- Worthily

APPENDIX 3
Use Descriptive Adjectives

Sometimes the right adjective is all you need to define the exact level of performance. Here are some you may find helpful:

A
- Absolute
- Abundant
- Acceptable
- Accountable
- Accurate
- Active
- Actual
- Adaptable
- Adept
- Affirmative
- Alert
- Almost
- Ambitious
- Analytical
- Answerable
- Articulate
- At-fault
- Authoritative

B
- Basic
- Belated
- Best
- Biased
- Bigoted
- Blameworthy

C
- Calm
- Capable
- Challenging
- Charismatic
- Clear
- Clear-thinking
- Cohesive
- Compelling
- Competent
- Complete
- Composed
- Comprehensive

- ❑ Concise
- ❑ Confident
- ❑ Conscientious
- ❑ Considerable
- ❑ Consistent
- ❑ Constructive
- ❑ Cooperative
- ❑ Courageous
- ❑ Creative
- ❑ Culpable
- ❑ Curious

D

- ❑ Decisive
- ❑ Dedicated
- ❑ Definite
- ❑ Dependable
- ❑ Desirable
- ❑ Determined
- ❑ Diligent
- ❑ Diplomatic
- ❑ Direct
- ❑ Discreet
- ❑ Distinctive
- ❑ Distorted
- ❑ Dogmatic
- ❑ Dynamic

E

- ❑ Eager
- ❑ Easy

- ❑ Effective
- ❑ Efficient
- ❑ Effortless
- ❑ Elementary
- ❑ Energetic
- ❑ Enlightening
- ❑ Enterprising
- ❑ Enthusiastic
- ❑ Entry-level
- ❑ Ethnocentric
- ❑ Exact
- ❑ Excellent
- ❑ Exceptional
- ❑ Exciting
- ❑ Extra
- ❑ Extraordinary
- ❑ Extreme

F

- ❑ Factual
- ❑ Fair
- ❑ Fast
- ❑ Favorable
- ❑ Fine
- ❑ Flawless
- ❑ Flexible
- ❑ Fluent
- ❑ Forceful
- ❑ Foremost
- ❑ Formidable

G

- ❑ General
- ❑ Generous
- ❑ Genuine
- ❑ Graceful
- ❑ Great

H

- ❑ Hands-on
- ❑ Handy
- ❑ Harmonious
- ❑ Heads-up
- ❑ Helpful
- ❑ Highest
- ❑ High-grade
- ❑ High-level
- ❑ High-tech
- ❑ Honest

I

- ❑ Ill-advised
- ❑ Ill-conceived
- ❑ Imaginative
- ❑ Immediate
- ❑ Immense
- ❑ Impeccable
- ❑ Important
- ❑ Independent
- ❑ Industrious
- ❑ Influential
- ❑ Informative

- ❏ Ingenious
- ❏ Innocent
- ❏ Innovative
- ❏ Instant
- ❏ Instinctive
- ❏ Instrumental
- ❏ Intelligent
- ❏ Intense
- ❏ Intent
- ❏ Intentional
- ❏ Interactive
- ❏ Intermittent
- ❏ Intolerant
- ❏ Inventive
- ❏ Involved

J

- ❏ Judicial
- ❏ Judicious
- ❏ Just
- ❏ Justifiable

K

- ❏ Keen
- ❏ Kind
- ❏ Knowing
- ❏ Knowledgeable

L

- ❏ Lasting
- ❏ Latent
- ❏ Latest

- ❏ Logical
- ❏ Loyal

M

- ❏ Magnificent
- ❏ Major
- ❏ Masterful
- ❏ Mature
- ❏ Maximum
- ❏ Meaningful
- ❏ Mechanical
- ❏ Methodical
- ❏ Meticulous
- ❏ Motivated

N

- ❏ Narrow-minded
- ❏ Natural
- ❏ Neat
- ❏ Normal

O

- ❏ Objective
- ❏ Observant
- ❏ Obvious
- ❏ Occasional
- ❏ Official
- ❏ Opinionated
- ❏ Opportunistic
- ❏ Optimal
- ❏ Orderly
- ❏ Organized

- ❏ Original
- ❏ Outstanding

P

- ❏ Painless
- ❏ Parochial
- ❏ Partial
- ❏ Particular
- ❏ Patient
- ❏ Perfect
- ❏ Periodical
- ❏ Persevering
- ❏ Persistent
- ❏ Persuasive
- ❏ Petulant
- ❏ Pleasant
- ❏ Poised
- ❏ Polite
- ❏ Positive
- ❏ Powerful
- ❏ Practical
- ❏ Pragmatic
- ❏ Precise
- ❏ Predictable
- ❏ Preeminent
- ❏ Premier
- ❏ Proactive
- ❏ Productive
- ❏ Professional
- ❏ Profound

- ❑ Progressive
- ❑ Prolific
- ❑ Prominent
- ❑ Proper
- ❑ Punctual

Q

- ❑ Quality
- ❑ Quantum
- ❑ Questionable
- ❑ Quick
- ❑ Quizzical
- ❑ Quotidian

R

- ❑ Rapid
- ❑ Rational
- ❑ Ready
- ❑ Realistic
- ❑ Reasonable
- ❑ Reassuring
- ❑ Regular
- ❑ Relentless
- ❑ Reliable
- ❑ Remarkable
- ❑ Repeat
- ❑ Repeatable
- ❑ Resilient
- ❑ Resourceful
- ❑ Respectful
- ❑ Responsible

- ❑ Responsive
- ❑ Rigorous
- ❑ Routine
- ❑ Rudimentary

S

- ❑ Safe
- ❑ Satisfactory
- ❑ Self-confident
- ❑ Serious
- ❑ Sharp
- ❑ Significant
- ❑ Simple
- ❑ Sincere
- ❑ Sizable
- ❑ Skillful
- ❑ Smooth
- ❑ Solid
- ❑ Sophisticated
- ❑ Sound
- ❑ Special
- ❑ Specific
- ❑ Splendid
- ❑ Spontaneous
- ❑ Sporadic
- ❑ State-of-the-art
- ❑ Steadfast
- ❑ Steady
- ❑ Stellar
- ❑ Stern

- ❑ Stimulating
- ❑ Straight
- ❑ Straightforward
- ❑ Straight-shooting
- ❑ Strategic
- ❑ Strict
- ❑ Stringent
- ❑ Strong
- ❑ Subjective
- ❑ Successful
- ❑ Succinct
- ❑ Sudden
- ❑ Superior
- ❑ Supportive
- ❑ Surprising
- ❑ Sustainable
- ❑ Swift
- ❑ Sympathetic
- ❑ Synergistic
- ❑ Systematic

T

- ❑ Tactful
- ❑ Tactical
- ❑ Tedious
- ❑ Thankful
- ❑ Thorough
- ❑ Thoughtful
- ❑ Time-constrained
- ❑ Time-honored

- ❑ Trustworthy
- ❑ Truthful
- ❑ Twisted
- ❑ Typical

U

- ❑ Ultimate
- ❑ Unexpected
- ❑ Uniform
- ❑ Unintentional
- ❑ Unique
- ❑ Unlimited
- ❑ Unmatched
- ❑ Unnecessary
- ❑ Unusual
- ❑ Urgent
- ❑ Useful
- ❑ Usual
- ❑ Utmost

V

- ❑ Valuable
- ❑ Verbal
- ❑ Versatile
- ❑ Viable
- ❑ Vibrant
- ❑ Victorious
- ❑ Vigorous
- ❑ Voluntary

W

- ❑ Warped
- ❑ Well-conceived
- ❑ Well-liked
- ❑ Well-worn
- ❑ Willful
- ❑ Willing
- ❑ Winning
- ❑ Worthwhile
- ❑ Worthy

X

- ❑ Xenophobic

Y

- ❑ Yearly
- ❑ Yeoman-like
- ❑ Yielding
- ❑ Youthful

Z

- ❑ Zen-like
- ❑ Zippy
- ❑ Zonked

About the Author

Sandra E. Lamb began her career in the field of technical writing, then moved on to a progression of organizational management and CEO positions. Along the way she developed and administered performance review and employee bonus programs that helped both her organization and her employees succeed.

Lamb has researched and written texts in business organization and management, and brings to *3000 Power Words and Phrases for Effective Performance Reviews* the kind of lightening accuracy and expert feel for the most effective words and phrases she demonstrated in her award-winning book, *How to Write It*, now in its third edition. She is also the author of *Personal Notes* and *Write the Right Words*.

For more information, or if you are interested in having her as a speaker, spokesperson, or consultant, visit SandraLamb.com.

Index

Also by Sandra E. Lamb

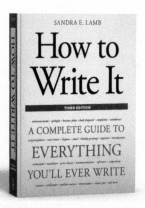

HOW TO WRITE IT, Third Edition
A Complete Guide to Everything You'll Ever Write
$18.99 paperback (Canada: $20.99)
ISBN: 978-1-60774-032-2
eBook ISBN: 978-1-60774-048-3

Available from TEN SPEED PRESS
wherever books are sold
www.tenspeed.com